pg 7

Jesus Complex
Was He Crazy, A Pathological Liar, Or The Son Of God?
pg 19

Mona Lisa's Smirk
The Truth Behind The Da Vinci Conspiracy
pg 30

Jesus.doc
Is The New Testament Reliable?
pg 42

The Path Laid By Prophets
Was The Messiah's Identity Encrypted Within
Ancient Hebrew Prophecy?
pg 59

Body Count
Is There Evidence That Jesus Rose From The Dead?
pg 72

Why Jesus?
Is He Relevant Today?
pg 80

FROM THE EDITORS

"What person in all of history would you like to meet?" Jack Black and Kyle Gass of Tenacious D were asked that question in an interview with *Esquire* magazine. Gass responded, "Who we'd like to meet? Jesus."

Black answered in a radically different way. Responding to his partner, he said, "You should say 'I' instead of 'we.' You'd find out he's just a dude....You'd want to know the answer to everything, and he'd say, 'How should I know? I'm just Jesus.'"[1]

Backpacker magazine surveyed more than 2,000 of its readers, asking them who they would most like to take a hike with. Angelina Jolie came out on top; Jesus was down the list at 37th. Maybe the readers of *Backpacker* couldn't picture Jesus in hiking boots (though more likely they were picturing Jolie in them).

If we could go back in time and meet the real Jesus, could we picture him in hiking boots? Would he be adventurous? Would he be cool and magnetic or dull and religious? In *Gods That Fail*, Vinoth Ramachandra wrote, "The Jesus of the gospels, unlike the Jesus of religious sentimentalism, is gentle and tough, witty and serious, stern and tenderhearted. The one thing the people who met him could not do was to stereotype him."[2]

Jesus is still front-page news after 20 centuries. In a lawsuit against the Vatican, an Italian judge must decide in early 2006 whether Jesus actually existed, or was an invention of the Catholic Church. Yet in a *Newsweek* magazine poll taken in 2004, a whopping 82% of American adults believe Jesus is God or the Son of God.[3]

Furthermore, in 2004, *Newsweek*, *Time*, *U.S. News & World Report*, *CNN*, *ABC News*, and *Fox News* all made Jesus Christ a feature story during the course of the year. At the same time, *The Passion of the Christ*, a movie about Jesus Christ, obliterated box office records. Why all this publicity? One would think that a man who lived 2,000 years ago would have virtually no relevance to our lives today.

Perhaps Jesus missed an opportunity to capitalize on his fame. Leslie Wylie, a columnist for *The Daily Beacon Online*, a publication of the University of Tennessee, remarked (with tongue in cheek) that Jesus "screwed up" by not copyrighting his name and likeness, since it has been hijacked by political opportunists.[4]

Why is it that we can calmly discuss so many issues, including spiritual and religious leaders, but when someone brings up the name of Jesus Christ, controversy breaks out, with no one turning the other cheek? The controversy over Jesus centers around the revolutionary words that he spoke. Not the lofty words he uttered on the Sermon on the Mount, which launched democracies, educational institutions, and set new standards for ethics and morality in the Western world. But the words that have stirred emotions are his radical claims – claims that separate him from all other religious leaders. Claims that if true---have profound implications on our lives, compelling us to respond.

So, who is the real Jesus? Is he "just a dude"? Did he even exist? If so, do we really know what he said and what he was like? Weren't the main accounts of his life written by his biased followers? If so, could the story of Jesus have been the most outrageous conspiracy of all time?

Several skeptics who initially assumed there was little or no evidence for Jesus Christ investigated the eyewitness accounts for reliability. In the following articles, we will investigate many of the skeptics' findings as well as explore answers to such questions as these: Did Jesus really exist? What did he say? Has there been a conspiracy to cover up the truth about Jesus, as the best-selling book *The Da Vinci Code* asserts?

How do we know if the eyewitness accounts about Jesus are accurate? Or did Constantine and early church leaders alter them? Did Jesus really die? Were Jesus and the Hebrew Messiah one and the same person, or was Jesus an imposter? Was Jesus merely a great man whom the church has deified? Or was he something more?

The only caveat for the investigation is this: we'll seek *judicial* evidence and not *scientific* evidence. Scientific evidence is that which can be duplicated in a lab. We do not think we can recreate the resurrection of Jesus in a petri dish. In a criminal case, circumstantial evidence provides sufficient confidence for a verdict to be rendered.

In this investigation we will be looking at the evidence, hearing from historians and other scholars about their conclusions. According to author and lecturer Ravi Zacharias, it is possible to link Jesus' words and his life to form a picture of truth. Zacharias writes, "This is precisely what makes Jesus unique. The whole range of both His life and His teaching can be subjected to the test of truth. Each aspect of His teaching is a link in the greater whole. Each facet is like the face of a diamond, catching the light as it is gently turned."[5]

As we examine the evidence available to us, we will see whether the pieces come together to form a clear picture of the extraordinary life and words of Jesus of Nazareth. And we will see if there is evidence to back up his radical claims.

ENDNOTES

[1] Quoted in Cal Fussman, "The Meaning of Life," *Esquire*, January 2004, 85.

[2] Vinoth Ramachandra, *Gods That Fail* (Carlisle, Cumbria, U.K.: Paternoster, 1996), 198.

[3] Jon Meacham, "The Birth of Jesus," *Newsweek*, December 13, 2004, 51.

[4] Leslie Wylie, "Jesus Should Copyright Name," *Daily Beacon Online*, http://dailybeacon.utk.edu/show-article.php?articleid=16686, April 1, 2005.

[5] Ravi Zacharias, *Jesus Among Other Gods* (Nashville: W, 2000), 55.

Born Identity

Was Jesus a real person?

"Well, I'm here to give the reality point of view, I guess," declared Ellen Johnson, president of American Atheists. "Because the reality is, there is not one shred of secular evidence there ever was a Jesus Christ. Jesus Christ and Christianity is a modern religion. And Jesus Christ is a compilation from other gods: Horas [sic], Mithras, who had the same origins, the same death as the mythological Jesus Christ."

Johnson and a blue-ribbon panel of religious leaders were discussing the question, "What happens after we die?" on a *Larry King Live* CNN broadcast. The usually unflappable King paused reflectively and then replied, "So you don't believe there was a Jesus Christ?"

With an air of certainty, Johnson responded, "There was not. It is not what I believe; there is no secular evidence that JC, Jesus Christ, ever existed."

King had no follow-up and went to a commercial break. No discussion of any evidence for or against Jesus' existence was forthcoming. The international television audience was left wondering.[1]

Fifty years earlier, in his book *Why I Am Not a Christian*, atheist Bertrand Russell shocked his generation by questioning Jesus' existence. He wrote: "Historically it is quite doubtful whether Christ ever existed at all, and if He did we do not know anything about Him, so that I am not concerned with the historical question, which is a very difficult one."[2]

Is it possible that the Jesus so many believe to be real never existed? In *The Story of Civilization*, secular historian Will Durant posed this question: "Did Christ exist? Is the life story of the founder of Christianity the product of human sorrow, imagination, and hope—a myth comparable to the legends of Krishna, Osiris, Attis, Adonis, Dionysus, and Mithras?"[3] Durant pointed out how the story of Christianity has "many suspicious resemblances to the legends of pagan gods."[4]

So, how can we know for sure that this man, whom many worship and others curse, was real? Is Johnson right when she asserts that Jesus Christ is a "compilation from other gods"? And is Russell right when he says that Jesus' existence is "quite doubtful"?

MYTH VS. REALITY

Let's begin with a more foundational question: What distinguishes myth from reality? How do we know, for example, that Alexander the Great really existed? Supposedly, in 336 B.C., Alexander the Great became king of Macedonia at 20 years of age. A military genius, this handsome, arrogant leader butchered his way through villages, towns, and kingdoms of the Greco-Persian world until he ruled it all. In a short eight years Alexander's armies had traversed a total of 22,000 miles in his conquests.

It has been said of Alexander that he cried when he ran out of worlds to conquer. (I'm thinking, this is not the person I want to play Monopoly with.)

Before he died at age 32, Alexander reportedly accomplished greater military deeds than anyone in history, not only of the kings who had lived

EVERYSTUDENT.COM

A SAFE PLACE TO EXPLORE QUESTIONS ABOUT GOD

before him, but also of those who followed, down to our own time. But today, other than cities named Alexandria, a boring film by Oliver Stone, and a few books, his legacy is all but forgotten. In fact, the name Colin Farrell had more drawing power at the box office than Alexander's.

In spite of the box office flop, historians cite three primary reasons they believe Alexander really existed:

- written documentation from early historians
- historical impact
- historical and archaeological evidence

HISTORICAL DOCUMENTS ABOUT JESUS

The historicity of Alexander the Great and his military conquests is drawn from five ancient sources, none of whom were eyewitnesses. Although written 400 years after Alexander, Plutarch's *Life of Alexander* is the primary account of his life.

Since Plutarch and the other writers were several hundred years removed from the events of Alexander's life, they based their information on prior accounts. Of the twenty contemporary historical accounts on Alexander, not one survives. Later accounts exist, but each presents a different "Alexander," with much left to our imagination. But regardless of the time gap of several hundred years, historians are convinced that Alexander was a real man and that the essential details of what we read about his life are true.

Keeping Alexander as a reference point, we'll note that for Jesus there are both religious and secular historical accounts. But we must ask the question, were they written by reliable and objective historians? Let's take a brief look.

THE NEW TESTAMENT

The 27 New Testament books claim to be written by authors who either knew Jesus or received firsthand knowledge of him from others. The four Gospel accounts record Jesus' life and words from different perspectives. These accounts have been heavily scrutinized by scholars both inside Christianity and outside it.

Even New Testament critic John Dominic Crossan of the Jesus Seminar believes that Jesus Christ really lived.

The consensus of most historians is that the Gospel accounts give us a clear picture of Jesus Christ. Whether the New Testament accounts are trustworthy is the subject of another article (See "Jesus.doc").

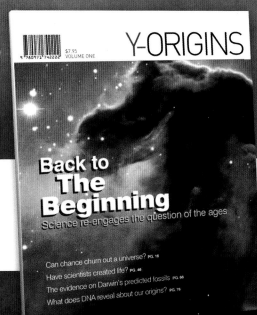

To confirm Jesus' existence we need to hear the opinions of non-Christian historians during Jesus' time as well as today. We also need to measure the historical impact of his life.

EARLY NON-CHRISTIAN ACCOUNTS

So, which first-century historians who wrote of Jesus did not have a Christian agenda? First of all, let's look to Jesus' enemies.

His Jewish opponents had the most to gain by denying Jesus' existence. But the evidence points in the opposite direction. "Several Jewish writings also tell of His flesh-and-blood existence. Both Gemaras of the Jewish Talmud refer to Jesus. Although these consist of only a few brief, bitter passages intended to discount Jesus' deity, these very early Jewish writings don't begin to hint that he was not a historical person."[5]

Flavius Josephus was a noted Jewish historian who began writing under Roman authority in 67 A.D.. Josephus, who was born just a few years after Jesus died, would have been keenly aware of Jesus' reputation among both Romans and Jews. In his famous *Antiquities of the Jews* (93 A.D.), Josephus wrote of Jesus as a real person. "At that time lived Jesus, a holy man, if man he may be called, for he performed wonderful works, and taught men, and joyfully received the truth. And he was followed by many Jews and many Greeks.

"Regardless of what anyone may personally think or believe about him, Jesus of Nazareth has been the dominant figure in the history of Western culture for almost twenty centuries...."

Jaroslav Pelikan, Yale historian

He was the Messiah."[6] Although there is dispute about some of the wording in the account, especially the reference to Jesus being the Messiah (scholars are skeptical, thinking that Christians inserted this phrase), certainly Josephus confirmed his existence.

What about secular historians—those who lived in ancient times but weren't religiously motivated? There is current confirmation of at least 19 early secular writers who made references to Jesus as a real person.[7]

One of antiquity's greatest historians, Cornelius Tacitus, affirmed that Jesus had suffered under Pilate. Tacitus was born around 25 years after Jesus died, and he had seen the spread of Christianity begin to impact Rome. The Roman historian wrote negatively of Christ and Christians, identifying them in 115 A.D. as "a race of men detested for their evil practices, and commonly called Chrestiani. The name was derived from Chrestus, who, in the reign of Tiberius, suffered under Pontius Pilate, Procurator of Judea."[8]

The following facts about Jesus were written by early non-Christian sources:

- Jesus was from Nazareth.
- Jesus lived a wise and virtuous life.
- Jesus was crucified in Palestine under Pontius Pilate during the reign of Tiberius Caesar at Passover time, being considered the Jewish king.

- Jesus was believed by his disciples to have died and risen from the dead three days later.
- Jesus' enemies acknowledged that he performed unusual feats they called "sorcery."
- Jesus' small band of disciples multiplied rapidly, spreading as far as Rome.
- Jesus' disciples denied polytheism, lived moral lives, and worshiped Christ as God.

Theologian Norman Geisler remarked, "This general outline is perfectly congruent with that of the New Testament."[9] All of these independent accounts, religious and secular, speak of a real man who matches up well with the Jesus in the Gospels. *Encyclopedia Britannica* cites these various secular accounts of Jesus' life as convincing proof of his existence. "These independent accounts prove that in ancient times even the opponents of Christianity never doubted the historicity of Jesus."[10]

HISTORICAL IMPACT

An important distinction between a myth and a real person is how the figure impacts history. For example, the Olympic Games originated on Mount Olympus in Greece, home of the temple of the Greek god Zeus. But Zeus has not changed governments, laws, or ethics.

The historian Thomas Carlyle said, "No great man lives in vain. The history of the world is but the biography of great men."[11] As Carlyle notes, it is real people, not myths, who impact history.

As a real person, Alexander impacted history by his military conquests, altering nations, governments, and laws. But what of Jesus Christ and his impact on our world?

The first-century governments of Israel and Rome were largely untouched by Jesus' life. The average Roman didn't know he existed until many years after his death, Roman culture remained largely aloof from his teaching for decades. It would be several centuries before killing Christians in the coliseum became a national pastime. The rest of the world had little, if any, knowledge of him. Jesus marshaled no army. He didn't write a book or change any laws. The Jewish leaders hoped to wipe out any memory of him, and it appeared they would succeed.

Today, however, ancient Rome lies in ruins. Caesar's mighty legions and the pomp of Roman imperial power have faded into oblivion. Yet how is Jesus remembered today? What is *his* enduring influence?

- More books have been written about Jesus than about any other person in history.
- Nations have used his words as the bedrock of their governments. According to Durant, "The triumph of Christ was the beginning of democracy."[12]
- His Sermon on the Mount established a new paradigm in ethics and morals.
- Schools, hospitals, and humanitarian works have been founded in his name. Harvard, Yale, Princeton, and Oxford are but a few universities that have Christians to thank for their beginning.

- The elevated role of women in Western culture traces its roots back to Jesus. (Women in Jesus' day were considered inferior and virtual nonpersons until his teaching was followed.)
- Slavery was abolished in Britain and America due to Jesus' teaching that each human life is valuable.
- Former drug and alcohol dependents, prostitutes, and others seeking purpose in life claim him as the explanation for their changed lives.
- Two billion people call themselves Christians. While some are Christian in name only, others continue to impact our culture by teaching Jesus' principles that all life is valuable and we are to love one another.

Remarkably, Jesus made all of this impact as a result of just a three-year period of public ministry. If Jesus didn't exist, one must wonder how a myth could so alter history. When world historian H. G. Wells was asked who has left the greatest legacy on history, he replied, "By this test Jesus stands first."[13]

Documentary evidence and historical impact point to the fact that Jesus did exist. If Jesus did really exist, we also would expect to discover his footprints imprinted within the details of history. Myths don't leave such confirming details.

TANGIBLE EVIDENCE

Despite the scrupulously historical film *Elf*, a trip to the North Pole quickly puts the myth label on Santa Claus. And in spite of Tom Hanks's assertions of Santa's reality in the movie *Polar Express*, all there is at the North Pole is ice. No reindeer or toy factories. No little men in red suits. The evidence of confirming details just isn't there. (Please keep the contents of this magazine away from minors.)

The details of Alexander's life, however, are chronicled by Plutarch and other historians, providing evidence of his existence. The aftermath of his conquests resulted in more than 70 cities being named Alexandria.

Names of his generals, places he conquered, and other details known to history paint a picture of a real person.

Yet the extensive details surrounding the life of Jesus Christ far surpass those of Alexander. The following details have convinced most scholars that Jesus did exist:

- historical New Testament sites
- confirmation of New Testament characters
- suddenness of Christianity's rise

One skeptic who thought Jesus was a myth was British journalist Malcolm Muggeridge. But on a television assignment to Israel, Muggeridge was faced with evidence about Jesus Christ that he didn't know existed. As he checked out historical places—Jesus' birthplace, Nazareth, the crucifixion site, and the empty tomb—a sense of Jesus' reality began to emerge.

Later he stated, "It was while I was in the Holy Land for the purpose of making three B.B.C. television programmes on the New Testament that a ... certainty seized me about Jesus' birth, ministry and Crucifixion. ... I became aware that there really had been a man, Jesus, who was also God."[14]

Some German higher-critical scholars in the 18th and 19th centuries had questioned Jesus' existence, stating that such key figures as Pontius Pilate and chief priest Joseph Caiaphas in the Gospel accounts had never been confirmed as real. No rebuttal was possible until the mid-20th century.

Archaeologists in 1962 confirmed Pilate's existence when they discovered his name included in an inscription on an excavated stone. Likewise, the existence of Caiaphas was uncertain until 1990, when an ossuary (bone box) was discovered bearing his inscription. Archaeologists have also discovered what they believe to be Simon Peter's house and a cave where John the Baptist did his baptizing.

Finally, perhaps the most convincing historical evidence that Jesus existed was the rapid rise of Christianity. How can it be explained without Christ? How could this group of fishermen and other working-men invent Jesus in a scant few years? Will Durant answered his own introductory question—did Christ exist?—with the following conclusion:

That a few simple men should in one generation have invented so powerful and appealing a personality, so lofty an ethic and so inspiring a vision of human brotherhood, would be a miracle far more incredible than any recorded in the Gospels. After two centuries of Higher Criticism the outlines of the life, character, and teaching of Christ, remain reasonably clear, and constitute the most fascinating feature in the history of Western man.[15]

One key for Durant and other scholars is the time factor. Myths and legends usually take hundreds of years to evolve—the story of George Washington never telling a lie was probably a lie, until two centuries turned it into legend. News of Christianity, on the other hand, took off faster than gossip about Brad and Jen's breakup. Had Jesus not existed, those who opposed Christianity would certainly have labeled him a myth from the outset. But they didn't.

Such evidence, along with the early written accounts and the historical impact of Jesus Christ, convince even skeptical historians that the founder of Christianity was neither myth nor legend. But one expert on myths wasn't so sure.

Like Muggeridge, Oxford scholar C. S. Lewis was initially convinced that Jesus was nothing more than a myth. Lewis once

stated, "All religions, that is, all mythologies ... are merely man's own invention—Christ as much as Loki."[16] (Loki is an old Norse god. Like Thor, but without the ponytail.)

Ten years after denouncing Jesus as a myth, Lewis discovered that historical details, including several eyewitness documents, verify his existence.

Jesus Christ has impacted history's landscape like a massive earthquake. And this earthquake has left a trail wider than the Grand Canyon. It is this trail of evidence that convinces scholars that Jesus really did exist and really did impact our world 2,000 years ago.

SCHOLARS' VERDICT

Clifford Herschel Moore, professor at Harvard University, remarked of Jesus'

historicity, "Christianity knew its Saviour and Redeemer not as some god whose history was contained in a mythical faith. … Jesus was a historical not a mythical being. No remote or foul myth obtruded itself on the Christian believer; his faith was founded on positive, historical, and acceptable facts."[17]

Few if any serious historians agree with Ellen Johnson's and Bertrand Russell's assertions that Jesus didn't exist. The extensive documentation of Jesus' life by contemporary writers, his profound historical impact, and the confirming tangible evidence of history have persuaded scholars that Jesus really did exist. Could a myth have done all that? All but a few extremely skeptical scholars say no.

Dr. Michael Grant of Cambridge has written, "To sum up, modern critical methods fail to support the Christ-myth theory. It has 'again and again been answered and annihilated by first rank scholars.' In recent years 'no serious scholar has ventured to postulate the non-historicity of Jesus.' "[18]

Yale historian Jaroslav Pelikan declared, "Regardless of what anyone may personally think or believe about him, Jesus of Nazareth has been the dominant figure in the history of Western culture for almost twenty centuries…. It is from his birth that most of the human race dates its calendars, it is by his name that millions curse and in his name that millions pray."[19]

NEWSFLASH

In February, 2006, a legal challenge to Jesus' existence wound up being thrown out of an Italian court. The plaintiff, Luigi Cascioli, 72, had argued his hometown priest and former schoolmate had effectively broken an Italian law by conning the public into believing that Jesus was a real person.

But instead of granting Cascioli his request to bring the case to court, the judge recommended magistrates investigate him for slandering priest Enrico Righi. Cascioli, author of a book called *The Fable of Christ*, said he would appeal to Italy's highest court, and then to The Hague.

Gospels in Brief

THE BIRTH

The Gospel writers all anchored their historical narratives in the Old Testament, beginning with messianic passages from the Hebrew prophets. These passages foretold the coming Messiah, using a fulfillment formula stating that "that" is "this." One such passage is Isaiah 9:6-7.

"A child is born to us, a son is given to us. And the government will rest on his shoulders. These will be his royal titles: Wonderful Counselor, Mighty God, Everlasting Father, Prince of Peace. His ever expanding, peaceful government will never end. He will rule forever with fairness and justice from the throne of his ancestor David." (Isaiah 9:6-7, NLT)

Roughly 700 years after Isaiah uttered this prophecy concerning the coming Messiah, the Gospels tell us, the long-awaited announcement is heralded by an angel. This angel came, not to awaiting multitudes, but to a lowly peasant woman, who was told she would birth the Savior, sans husband.

The young woman, Mary, was engaged to a village carpenter named Joseph. But when Mary told Joseph what the angel had spoken, explaining that she was already pregnant with the child, Joseph obviously assumed an illicit relationship and moved to quietly dissolve the marriage.

But the Gospel of Matthew tells us that an angelic messenger related to Joseph, in a dream, that what Mary had claimed was actually true. In fact, it must have been quite a dream, for it compelled him to believe Mary. In the history of unplanned pregnancies this was probably not the first time such a story was told. It was, in all likelihood, the first time it was believed.

The Gospels relate that the child was born in Bethlehem, this being the town of Joseph's origin. Everyone needed to return to their ancestral home to fulfill the requirements of a Roman census. As Bethlehem brimmed with returning pilgrims the family was forced to stay in a barn. Perhaps this was God's plan, or perhaps Joseph just *didn't* plan, but we are left viewing irony itself: Mary gave birth to a son, Jesus, and laid the world's Messiah in a feeding trough for animals.

THE WONDER YEARS

The childhood of Jesus truly was the "wonder years," for the Gospels, in their silence, leave us to wonder what transpired. Only one story of Jesus' youth is preserved, in which his parents (Joseph and Mary) having lost him, discovered him in the Temple discussing the things of God with the religious leaders—a hint of things to come.

Other than this Temple incident and the details surrounding his birth, many have wondered why the early years in Jesus' life are largely unaccounted for. But the reasons are relatively easy to understand.

Since Jesus' public ministry didn't begin until he was approximately 30 years of age, there would be virtually nothing in his early years of consequence to write about. None of the miracles he performed or sermons he preached occurred until then. Additionally, his apostles, the authors of the New Testament, weren't there to witness his pre-ministry life, not joining Jesus until he began his public ministry.

PUBLIC MINISTRY

At about the age of 30, Jesus went to Nazareth, where he had been brought up, and on the Sabbath day he went into the synagogue, as was his custom. As he stood to do the Scripture reading, the scroll of the prophet Isaiah was handed to him. Unrolling it, he found the place where it was written:

> The Spirit of the Lord is upon me, for he has appointed me to preach Good News to the poor. He has sent me to proclaim that captives will be released, that the blind will see, that the downtrodden will be freed from their oppressors, and that the time of the Lord's favor has come. (Luke 4:18-19, NLT)

He rolled up the scroll, handed it back to the attendant, and sat down. Everyone in the synagogue stared at him intently. Then he said, "This Scripture has come true today before your very eyes!" (Luke 4:20-21, NLT)

This, according to the Gospel of Luke, marked the beginning of Jesus' public ministry. The Isaiah passage from which he read refers to the coming Messiah, and by declaring, "This Scripture has come true," Jesus began his ministry with a gunshot summoning the attention of all Israel and beginning a race that would last roughly three years before it ended in a state-sponsored lynching.

One would assume that Jesus' teaching was quite diverse, addressing all of the many social and moral injustices of his day. This was not the case. With the exception

of the Sermon on the Mount, Jesus taught one primary message: "The kingdom of God is upon you, and I am its king."

The ministry of Jesus was laced with miracles, but every miracle was an object lesson, a 30-second commercial promoting that one central message.

For example, in the Old Testament, the prophet Isaiah spoke of the Messiah's coming kingdom, describing it in these words: "In that day deaf people will hear words read from a book, and blind people will see through the gloom and darkness" and "When he comes, he will open the eyes of the blind and unstop the ears of the deaf" (Isaiah 29:18; 35:5). So every time Jesus gave sight to the blind and hearing to the deaf, it was freighted with messianic implications.

Besides telling of his messages and miracles to the masses, the Gospels draw us in to the inner circle of Jesus' most loyal, though flawed, group of followers: the disciples. Jesus assumed not just the role of Messiah, but that of mentor, training the disciples to carry on the proclamation of the kingdom—and its king—once the king had been killed.

DEATH AND RESURRECTION

The ministry of Jesus ended as abruptly as it had begun. Upon his final visit to Jerusalem for the Passover, Jesus told his 12 closest disciples that he would be betrayed, arrested, and crucified but also that he would come back to life three days later. Jesus' followers were confused, for it seemed inconceivable that the Messiah's reign

should end in death. In fact, Jesus saw his death as inaugurating his reign. But these were details to be worked out later, as upon entering Jerusalem, the mechanisms of betrayal were already in high gear and there was no time left to clarify.

As Jesus predicted, he was betrayed by one of his own disciples—Judas Iscariot—and arrested. In a mock trial under the Roman governor Pontius Pilate (to whom the Jewish leaders brought him since under Roman law they could not carry out their own executions), he was convicted of treason and condemned to die on a cross.

At 3:00 in the afternoon, after hanging on the cross for approximately six hours, Jesus cried out, "It is finished." And with that breathed his last breath.

The Gospels declare that three days later reports began to spread of witnesses who had seen Jesus. As the number of witnesses grew to several hundred, Jerusalem was in an uproar. It was divided and would remain so—Christianity had been birthed.

ENDNOTES

[1] Ellen Johnson and Larry King, "What Happens After We Die?" *Larry King Live*, CNN, April 14, 2005.

[2] Bertrand Russell, *Why I Am Not a Christian* (New York: Simon & Schuster, 1957), 16.

[3] Will Durant, *Caesar and Christ*, vol. 3 of The Story of Civilization (New York: Simon & Schuster, 1972), 553.

[4] Ibid., 557.

[5] D. James Kennedy, *Skeptics Answered* (Sisters, OR: Multnomah, 1997), 76. The Gemaras are early rabbinical commentaries of the Jewish Talmud, a body of theological writings, dated a.d. 200–500.

[6] Quoted in Durant, 554.

[7] Durant, 73.

[8] Quoted in Durant, 281.

[9] Norman Geisler and Peter Bocchino, *Unshakable Foundations* (Grand Rapids, MI: Bethany House, 2001), 269.

[10] Quoted in Josh McDowell, *Evidence That Demands a Verdict*, vol. 1 (Nashville: Nelson, 1979), 87.

[11] Quoted in Christopher Lee, *This Sceptred Isle*, 55 B.C.–1901 (London: Penguin, 1997), 1.

[12] Will Durant, *The Story of Philosophy* (New York: Pocket, 1961), 428.

[13] Quoted in Bernard Ramm, *Protestant Christian Evidences* (Chicago: Moody Press, 1957), 163.

[14] Malcolm Muggeridge, *Jesus Rediscovered* (Bungay, Suffolk, U.K.: Fontana, 1969), 8.

[15] Durant, Caesar and Christ, Ibid.

[16] David C. Downing, *The Most Reluctant Convert* (Downers Grove, IL: InterVarsity, 2002), 57.

[17] Quoted in McDowell, 193.

[18] Michael Grant, *Jesus* (London: Rigel, 2004), 200.

[19] Jaroslav Pelikan, *Jesus through the Centuries* (New York: Harper & Row, 1987), 1.

JC

Jesus Complex

WAS HE CRAZY, A PATHOLOGICAL LIAR, OR THE SON OF GOD?

Have you ever met somebody with such personal magnetism that they are always the center of attention? Possibly their personality or intelligence---but something about them is enigmatic. Well, that's the way it was two thousand years ago with Jesus Christ. But what makes Jesus relevant even today into the 21st century are the claims he made about himself.

As an unheralded carpenter from an obscure village in Palestine, Jesus made claims that, if true, have profound implications on our lives. According to Jesus, you and I are special, part of a grand cosmic scheme.

It was primarily Jesus' outrageous claims that caused him to be viewed as a crackpot by both the Roman authorities and the Jewish hierarchy. Although he was an outsider with no credentials or political powerbase, within three years, Jesus changed the world for the next 20 centuries. Other moral and religious leaders have left an

impact---but nothing like that unknown carpenter from Nazareth.

What was it about Jesus Christ that made the difference? Was he merely a great man, or something more?

These questions get to the heart of who Jesus really was. Some believe he was merely a great moral teacher; others believe he was simply the leader of the world's greatest religion. But many believe something far more. Christians believe that God has actually visited us in human form. And they believe the evidence backs that up. So who is the real Jesus? Let's take a closer look.

As we take a deeper look at the world's most controversial person, we begin by asking: could Jesus have been merely a great moral teacher?

GREAT MORAL TEACHER?

Almost all scholars acknowledge that Jesus was a great moral teacher. In fact, his brilliant insight into human morality is an accomplishment recognized even by those of other religions. In his book *Jesus of Nazareth*, Jewish scholar Joseph Klausner wrote, "It is universally admitted … that Christ taught the purest and sublimest ethics … which throws the moral precepts and maxims of the wisest men of antiquity far into the shade."[1]

Jesus' Sermon on the Mount has been called the most superlative teaching of human ethics ever uttered by an individual. In fact, much of what we know today as "equal rights" actually is the result of Jesus' teaching. Historian Will Durant said of Jesus that "he lived and struggled unremittingly for 'equal rights'; in modern times he would have been sent to Siberia. 'He that is greatest among you, let him be your servant'—this is the inversion of all political wisdom, of all sanity."[2]

Some have tried to separate Jesus' teaching on ethics from his claims about himself, believing that he was simply a great man who taught lofty moral principles. This was the approach of one of America's Founding Fathers.

President Thomas Jefferson, ever the enlightened rationalist, sat down in the White House with two identical copies of the New Testament, a straight-edge razor, and a sheaf of octavo-size paper. Over

LEADERSHIP UNIVERSITY

THE MEETING PLACE OF FAITH AND REASON.
UNIVERSITY PROFESSORS FROM ACROSS THE
COUNTRY WRITE FROM THEIR VARIOUS DISCIPLINES ON
GOD, SCIENCE, FAITH, AND INTELLIGENT DESIGN.

WWW.LeaderU.COM

the course of a few nights, he made quick work of cutting and pasting his own Bible, a slim volume he called "The Philosophy of Jesus of Nazareth." After slicing away every passage that suggested Jesus' divine nature, Jefferson had a Jesus who was no more and no less than a good, ethical guide.[3]

Thus Jefferson had reinvented Jesus to his own liking. In fact, he liked Jesus' ethical teaching about human equality so much that he used it in the Declaration of Independence in which he wrote, "We hold these truths to be self-evident, that all men are created equal…."

But it was not Jesus' lofty moral and ethical teaching that polarized his enemies and altered 2000 years of history. In fact, as we will see, if Jesus' claims about himself weren't true, then he couldn't have been a great moral teacher. For that reason some merely call Jesus a great religious leader. Perhaps flawed, they may argue, but nonetheless, great.

GREAT RELIGIOUS LEADER?

Does the title, "great religious leader" best describe Jesus Christ? Surprisingly, Jesus never claimed to be a religious leader. He never got into religious politics or pushed an ambitious agenda, and he ministered almost entirely outside the established religious framework.

> "Then comes the real shock. Among these Jews there suddenly turns up a man who goes about talking as if he was God. He claims to forgive sins. He says He always existed. He says He is coming to judge the world at the end of time."
>
> C. S. Lewis, Oxford scholar

When one compares Jesus with the other great religious leaders, a remarkable distinction emerges. Ravi Zacharias, who grew up in a Hindu culture, has studied world religions and observed a fundamental distinction between other religious founders and Jesus Christ.

> Whatever we may make of their claims, one reality is inescapable. They are teachers who point to their teaching or show some particular way. In all of these, there emerges an instruction, a way of living. It is not Zoroaster to whom you turn; it is Zoroaster to whom you listen. It is not Buddha who delivers you; it is his Noble Truths that instruct you. It is not Mohammad who transforms you; it is the beauty of the Koran that woos you. By contrast, Jesus did not only teach or expound His message. He was identical with His message.[4]

The truth of Zacharias's point is underscored by the number of times in the Gospels that Jesus' teaching message was simply "Come to me" or "Follow me" or "Obey me." Also, Jesus made it clear that his primary mission was to forgive sins, something only God could do.

No other major religious leader ever claimed the power to forgive sins. And according to Huston Smith in *The World's Great Religions*, Jesus distinguished himself even further. Smith writes,

> Only two people ever astounded their contemporaries so much that the question they evoked was not 'Who is he?' but '*What is he?*' They were Jesus and Buddha. The answers these two gave were exactly the opposite.
> Buddha said unequivocally that he was a mere man, not a god—almost as if he foresaw later attempts to worship him. Jesus, on the other hand, claimed … to be divine.[5]

DID JESUS CLAIM TO BE GOD?

Clearly, from the earliest years of the church, Jesus was called Lord and regarded by most Christians as God. Yet his divinity was a doctrine that was subjected to great debate. So the question—and it is *the* question—is this: Did Jesus really claim to be God (the Creator), or was his divinity something invented or assumed by the New Testament authors?

Some scholars believe Jesus was such a powerful teacher and compelling personality that his disciples just assumed he was God. Or maybe they just wanted to think he was God. John Dominic Crossan and the Jesus Seminar (a fringe group of skeptical scholars with presuppositions against miracles) are among those who believe Jesus was deified in error.

Others who say he didn't claim to be God include Jehovah's Witnesses, Christian Scientists, Unitarians, and a few other religious groups outside the borders of traditional Christianity.

Christians insist that Jesus did claim deity. As a deist, Thomas Jefferson had no problem accepting Jesus' teachings on morals and ethics while denying his deity.[6] But as we've said, and will explore further, if Jesus was not who he claimed to be, then we must examine some other alternatives, none of which would make him a great moral teacher.

Even a superficial reading of the Gospels reveals that Jesus claimed to be someone more than a prophet like Moses or Daniel. But it is the nature of those claims that concern us. Two questions are worthy of attention.

- Did Jesus actually claim to be God?
- When he said "God," did Jesus really mean he was the Creator of the universe spoken of in the Hebrew Bible?

To address these questions, let's consider Jesus' words in Matthew 28:18, NLT: "I have been given complete authority in heaven and on earth."

What did Jesus mean when he claimed to have complete authority in heaven and on earth?

"Authority" was a well-understood term in Roman-occupied Israel. At that time, Caesar was the supreme authority in the entire Roman world. His edict could instantly launch legions for war, condemn or exonerate criminals, and establish laws and rules of government. In fact, Caesar's authority was such that he himself claimed divinity.

So, at the very least Jesus was claiming authority on a par with Caesar himself. But He didn't just say he had *more* authority than the Jewish leaders or Roman rulers; Jesus was claiming to be *the supreme authority* in the universe. To those he spoke to, it meant that he was God. Not *a* god—but *the* God.

According to former skeptic and Oxford professor, C. S. Lewis, Jesus' claim to be God hit both his followers and enemies like a thunderbolt:

'Then comes the real shock,' wrote Lewis: 'Among these Jews there suddenly turns up a man who goes about talking as if He was God. He claims to forgive sins. He says He always existed. He says He is coming to judge the world at the end of time.'[7]

DID JESUS CLAIM TO BE THE CREATOR?

But is it possible that Jesus was just reflecting God's authority and was not stating that he was the actual Creator? At first glance that seems plausible. Yet Jesus' claim to have all authority seems to make sense only if he is the Creator of the universe. The word "all" encompasses everything---including creation itself.

As we look deeper into Jesus' own words, a pattern seems to emerge. Jesus made radical assertions about himself that, if true, unmistakably point to his deity. Here is a partial list of such statements as recorded by eyewitness accounts.

- I am the resurrection and the life. (John 11:25, NIV)
- I am the light of the world. (John 8:12, NIV)
- I and my Father are one. (John 10:30, NIV)
- I am the Alpha and the Omega, the First and the Last, the Beginning and the End. (Revelation 22:13, NIV)
- I am the way, the truth, and the life. (John 14:6, NIV)
- I am the only way to the Father [God]. (John 14:6)

Once again, we must go back to context. In the Hebrew Scriptures, when Moses asked God his name at the burning bush, God answered, "I AM." He was telling Moses that He is the only Creator, eternal and transcendent of time.

Since the time of Moses, no practicing Jew would ever refer to himself or anyone else by "I AM." As a result, Jesus' "I AM" claims infuriated the Jewish leaders. One time, for example, some leaders explained to Jesus why they were trying to kill him: "Because you, a mere man, have made yourself God" (John 10:33, NLT).

But the point here is not simply that such a phrase fumed the religious leaders. The point is that they knew exactly what he was saying—he was claiming to be God, the Creator of the universe. It is only this claim that would have brought the accusation of blasphemy. To read into the text that Jesus claimed to be God is clearly warranted, not simply by his words, but also by their reaction to those words.

Some who teach that we are all gods might accept Jesus' claims, as long as they weren't exclusive. The idea that we are all part of God, and that within us is the seed of divinity, is simply not a possible meaning for Jesus' words and actions. Such thoughts are revisionist, foreign to his teaching, foreign to his stated beliefs, and foreign to his disciples' understanding of his teaching.

Jesus taught that he is God in the way the Jews understood God and the way the Hebrew Scriptures portrayed God, not in the way the New Age movement understands God. Neither Jesus nor his audience had been weaned on *Star Wars*, and so when they spoke of God, they were not speaking of cosmic forces. It's simply bad history to redefine what Jesus meant by the concept of God.

There are many who just aren't able to accept Jesus as God, and want to call him a great moral teacher. But if Jesus wasn't God, are we still okay by calling him a great moral teacher? Lewis argued, "I am trying here to prevent anyone from saying the really foolish thing that people often say about Him: 'I'm ready to accept Jesus as a great moral teacher, but I don't accept his claim to be God.' That is the one thing we must not say."[8]

In his quest for truth, Lewis knew that he could not have it both ways with the identity of Jesus. Either Jesus was who he claimed to be—God in the flesh—or his claims were false. And if they were false, Jesus could not be a great moral teacher. He would either be lying intentionally or he would be a lunatic with a God complex.

So the options we must choose from for Jesus' true identity are:

- Jesus was a liar who knowingly deceived us.
- Jesus was a lunatic who was self-deceived.
- Jesus was who he claimed to be —God.

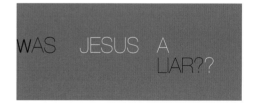

WAS JESUS A LIAR??

In the movie *Deceived*, Goldie Hawn plays the role of Adrienne Saunders, a recently widowed woman who sees fleeting glimpses of her late husband, Jack Saunders (John Heard). As the plot unfolds, Hawn realizes that her former husband had spun a web of deceit, faking his own death. She discovers that for years Saunders had been living under an assumed identity with another wife.

Few people have ever accused Jesus Christ of living a double life like Jack Saunders. Even most non-Christians believe Jesus was a good person. But if one examines his claims, then the issue that emerges is: either Jesus was the world's greatest deceiver, or he was exactly who he claimed to be. So which is the truth?

The question we must deal with is, what could possibly motivate Jesus to live his entire life as a lie? He taught that God was opposed to lying and hypocrisy, so he wouldn't have been doing it to please his Father. He certainly didn't lie for his followers' benefit. (All but one were martyred.) And so we are left with only two other reasonable explanations, each of which is problematic.

Many people have lied for personal gain. In fact, the motivation of most lies is some perceived benefit to oneself. What could Jesus have hoped to gain from lying about his identity? Power would be the most obvious answer. If people believed he was God, he would have tremendous power. (That is why many ancient leaders, such as the Caesars, claimed divine origin.)

The rub with this explanation is that Jesus shunned all attempts to move him in the direction of seated power, instead chastising those who abused such power and lived their lives pursuing it. He also chose to reach out to the outcasts (poor and hurting), those without power, creating a network of people whose influence was less than zero. In a way that could only be described as bizarre, all that Jesus did and said moved diametrically in the other direction from power.

It would seem that if power was Jesus' motivation, he would have avoided the cross at all costs. Yet, on several occasions, he told his disciples that the cross was his destiny and mission. How would dying on a Roman cross bring one power?

Death, of course, brings all things into proper focus. And while many martyrs have died for a cause they believed in, few have been willing to die for a known lie. Certainly all hopes for Jesus' own personal gain would have ended on the cross. Yet, to his last breath, he would not relinquish his claim of being the unique Son of God.

So if Jesus was above lying for personal benefit, perhaps his radical claims were falsified in order to leave a legacy. But the prospect of being beaten to a pulp and nailed to a cross would quickly dampen the enthusiasm of most would-be superstars.

Here is another haunting fact. If Jesus were to have simply dropped the claim of being God's Son, he never would have been condemned. It was his claim to be God and his unwillingness to recant of it that got him crucified.

Do historians believe Jesus lied? Scholars have scrutinized Jesus' words and life to see if there is any evidence of a defect in his moral character. In fact, even the most ardent skeptics are stunned by Jesus' moral and ethical purity. One of those was skeptic and antagonist John Stuart Mill (1806–73). Yet Mill called Jesus an "ideal representative and guide for humanity."[9]

According to historian Philip Schaff, there is no evidence, either in church history or in secular history, that Jesus lied about anything. Schaff argued, "How, in the name of logic, common sense, and experience, could a deceitful, selfish, depraved man have invented, and consistently maintained from the beginning to end, the purest and noblest character known in history with the most perfect air of truth and reality?"[10]

To go with the option of liar seems to swim upstream against everything Jesus taught, lived, and died for. To most scholars, it just doesn't make sense. Yet, to deny Jesus' claims, one must come up with some explanation. And if Jesus' claims are not true, and he wasn't lying, the only option remaining is that he must have been self-deceived.

OXFORD SKEPTIC CHECKS THE EVIDENCE:

Clive Staples Lewis was born in Belfast, Northern Ireland, in 1898. He graduated from University College, Oxford, in 1923. For 30 years he was a fellow and tutor in English at Magdalen College, Oxford. Then he went to Cambridge as professor of medieval and Renaissance English. Lewis was a brilliant lecturer who could speak spontaneously about Greek and Latin texts without notes.

Lewis regarded Christianity as just another myth. But another atheist, T. D. Weldon, had shocked him with a statement regarding the remarkable evidence for Jesus Christ. Lewis began a quest for truth that led him to believe in a God, but he still was unconvinced that Jesus was God. However, Lewis was greatly influenced by his friend J. R. R. Tolkien (author of The Lord of the Rings) and began to examine the rational basis for belief in Christianity. Together with Tolkien and Charles Williams, Lewis formed a literary group called the Inklings, in which the members had deep conversations about the difference between Christianity and myths. Although Christianity had a mythlike appearance, unlike myths and legends, it was backed by solid historical evidence, proving it to be true.

Lewis was a prolific author, writing The Chronicles of Narnia series, his autobiography, *Surprised by Joy*, *Mere Christianity*, and among his most substantial books, *English Literature in the Sixteenth Century*. In another work, *The Problem of Pain*, Lewis suggested that much of the suffering in the world can be traced to the evil choices people make.

In his own life, Lewis followed Christian principles. He gave away two-thirds of his income, sat at the bedside of the sick, and personally served the poor. The Chronicles of Narnia series has turned out to be the most lasting of Lewis's fictional works. Lewis died on November 22, 1963.

WAS JESUS A LUNATIC?

Albert Schweitzer, who was awarded the Nobel Prize in 1952 for his humanitarian efforts, had his own views about Jesus. Schweitzer concluded that insanity was behind Jesus' claim to be God. In other words, Jesus was wrong about his claims but didn't intentionally lie. According to this theory, Jesus was deluded into actually believing he was the Messiah.

As a skeptic, C. S. Lewis realized that Jesus was either a liar, a lunatic, or the real thing. He writes, "He would either be a lunatic—on a level with the man who says he is a poached egg—or else he would be the Devil of Hell."[11]

But even those most skeptical of Christianity rarely question Jesus' sanity. Social reformer William Channing (1780–1842), admittedly not a Christian, stated that the idea that Jesus was self-deluded is the most absurd title we could give him.[12] Nothing Jesus said or did point to any mental instability.

Even the great skeptic Rousseau, acknowledged Jesus' superior character and mental balance, writing, "What presence of mind. … Yes, if the life and death of Socrates are those of a philosopher, the life and death of Jesus Christ are those of a God."[13]

Schaff posed the question we must ask ourselves: "Is such an intellect—thoroughly healthy and vigorous, always ready and always self-possessed—liable to a radical and most serious delusion concerning his own character and mission?"[14]

So, was Jesus a liar or a lunatic, or was he the Son of God? Could Jefferson have been right by labeling Jesus "only a good moral teacher" while denying him deity? Interestingly, the audience who heard Jesus—both believers and enemies—never regarded him as a mere moral teacher. Jesus produced three primary effects in the people who met him: hatred, terror, or adoration.

It is the claims of Jesus Christ that force us to make a choice about who he is. We can't just cut and paste Jesus and his words, like Jefferson attempted to do. Lewis writes,

You must make your choice. Either this man was, and is, the Son of God: or else a madman or something worse. You can shut Him up for a fool, you can spit at Him and kill him as a demon or you can fall at his feet and call Him Lord and God. But let us not come with any patronizing nonsense about His being a great human teacher. He has not left that open to us. He did not intend to.[15]

The apostle Paul originally thought Jesus was an imposter, and as a Jewish leader, severely persecuted Christians. But later he came to a much different conclusion, as he writes to the young church at Philippi:

Though he was God….he appeared in human form. [16]

The entire message of Jesus' life and words is only valid if his claims about himself are true. If they are true, then his words about life and purpose command our utmost attention. As Lewis says, each of us must make our own choice about the most significant life who ever existed. Who do you say Jesus is?

"You must make your choice: Either this man was, and is, the Son of God: or else a madman or something worse.... But let us not come up with any patronizing nonsense about His being a great human teacher. He has not left that open to us."

C. S. Lewis, Oxford professor

ENDNOTES

[1] Quoted in Josh McDowell, *Evidence That Demands a Verdict*, vol. 1 (Nashville: Nelson, 1979), 127.

[2] Will Durant, *The Story of Philosophy* (New York: Washington Square, 1961), 428.

[3] Linda Kulman and Jay Tolson, "The Jesus Code," *U. S. News & World Report*, December 22, 2003, 1.

[4] Ravi Zacharias, *Jesus among Other Gods* (Nashville: Word, 2000), 89.

[5] Peter Kreeft and Ronald K. Tacelli, *Handbook of Christian Apologetics* (Downers Grove, IL: InterVarsity, 1994), 150.

[6] A deist is someone who believes in a standoffish God—a deity who created the world and then lets it run according to pre-established laws. Deism was a fad among intellectuals around the time of America's independence, and Jefferson bought into it.

[7] C. S. Lewis, *Mere Christianity* (San Francisco: HarperCollins, 1972), 51.

[8] Lewis, 52.

[9] Quoted in Josh McDowell, *The New Evidence That Demands a Verdict* (San Bernardino, CA: Here's Life, 1999), 159.

[10] Quoted in McDowell, *New Evidence*, 160.

[11] Lewis, 52.

[12] Quoted in McDowell, *New Evidence*, 161, 162.

[13] Quoted in McDowell, *New Evidence*, 122, 129.

[14] Quoted in McDowell, *New Evidence*, 162.

[15] Lewis, 52.

[16] Philippians 2: 6, 7

Washington, April 20.—Probably the oldest book of consecutive accounts kept by government officers is a time worn volume in the office of General Anson G. McCook, secretary of the senate, in which are recorded the compensation and mileage paid to each senator from the first session of the Second congress down to 1881—a round century of years. It is a leather bound book, two inches thick, of English make and with heavy leaves hand ruled and now yellow with age and service. It contains the accounts of every secretary of the senate since the inauguration of the government—there have only been eight secretaries altogether—and the attesting signature of every vice-president of the United States. In order to preserve the volume from dissolution and disfigurement, General McCook had it rebound and placed in a coarse canvas cover, where with proper care it ought to last several centuries longer. The ink is still clear, and the entries of names and figures are remarkable for their neatness.

When this book of accounts was opened in 1791 senators only got as much remuneration as their clerks get now a days—$6 a day. Their travelling expenses were paid to the extent of 30 cents for every mile travelled to and from the seat of government. Since then congress has changed the rate and amount of compensation eight times. The first change came in 1796 in the shape of an increase in the per diem allowance to $7 and in the mileage to 35 cents. This lasted but a year and then the old rates were restored. From 1816 to 1818 the experiment was tried of giving each senator an annual salary of $1,500 instead of a fixed sum per day, but apparently without success, for in the latter years congress went back to the per diem allowance, increasing it to $8. The mileage rate was also put at $8 instead of 35 cents. These rates continued in force until 1856, when senators were voted $3,000 a year and the same mileage. In 1866 the salary was increased to $5,000 and the mileage rate reduced to 20 cents. These are the rates now in force, but there was one year, serving as an equal interregnum, from 1870 to 1871, when senators were paid at the rate of $7,500, in addition to their actual travelling expenses.

It costs about six times as much to run our senators' car fare now as it did during Washington's first administration, although there are only about three times as many senators. The average amount thus expended then was about $5,000. Now it is in the neighborhood of $50,000. In 1852 it was $23,000 in round numbers and by 1851 it reached $33,000. In 1856 it grew to $27,500 and in 1861 Secretary McCook's book puts it at the enormous figure of $74,800. But about this time some senators had to do a good deal of travelling to get to and from Washington; Senator Joseph Lane, of Oregon, for instance, being accredited with getting over 14,820 miles of the earth's surface and receiving a check therefor to the amount of $5,908. Presumably, he charged up for the distance by way of Cape Horn, but whether he really got to the seat of government by that route or overland the ancient book does not tell. It took good sea legs as well as patriotism to be a Pacific coast senator in those days. But $6,000 seems a pretty good price for an excursion ticket from Oregon to the capital, even in 1860.

Complaint is frequently made that the present salary of senators is much too small. People here speak of senators who "live on their salaries" as they would speak of a peculiar physiognomy or a social phenomenon, such senators are so unusual. Those few who do are, as a rule, men who eschew society, who give no dinners, who live in second-class boarding houses or cheap hotels, and who are seldom heard of outside the senate chamber. I have in mind one notable exception among this class. His name is mentioned in the list of presidential candidates, he is one of the pillars of the senate, he is seen at most social gatherings, he is a great diner-out, polite and agreeable; yet people say that he lives on his $5,000 a year. But he gives no dinners himself in return for social compliments; lives in a boarding house and has only a small family to support. The cost of living in Washington is greater than in most towns where senators come and is constantly increasing. Rents are high in desirable parts of the town, and the member of congress who brings his family for a season at the capital and must and expects to entertain and to be entertained, even moderately finds his five thousand a year considerably less than a thousand if doing to get back of what

MONA LISA'S SMIRK

TRUTH

The Truth Behind the daVinci Conspiracy?

Emperor
Constantine
(306-337 A.D.)

• **Did Jesus have a secret marriage with Mary Magdalene?**

• **Was Jesus' divinity invented by Constantine and the church?**

• **Were the original records of Jesus destroyed?**

• **Do recently discovered manuscripts tell the truth about Jesus?**

Has a gigantic conspiracy resulted in the reinvention of Jesus? According to the book and movie, *The Da Vinci Code*, that is exactly what happened. Several of the book's assertions regarding Jesus smack of conspiracy. For example, the book states:

Nobody is saying Christ was a fraud, or denying that He walked the earth and inspired millions to better lives. All we are saying is that Constantine took advantage of Christ's substantial influence and importance. And in doing so, he shaped the face of Christianity as we know it today.[1]

Could this shocking assertion from Dan Brown's best-selling book be true? Or is the premise behind it just the stuff of a good

conspiracy novel—on par with a belief that aliens crash-landed at Roswell, New Mexico, or that there was a second gunman on the grassy knoll in Dallas when JFK was assassinated? Either way, the story is compelling. No wonder Brown's book has become one of the best-selling stories of the decade and is predicted to become one of the top movies of all time.

In *The Da Vinci Code* Brown mysteriously weaves a tapestry of fact and fiction throughout its exciting and suspenseful plot. In what Brown calls "the greatest conspiracy in the past 2000 years," *The Da Vinci Code* states that the real Jesus Christ was hijacked, and that his claim to be God is an invention. So has Brown uncovered the truth about Christianity, or has he twisted the facts? Let's take a look.

THE JESUS CONSPIRACY

The Da Vinci Code begins with the murder of a French museum curator named Jacques Saunière. A scholarly Harvard professor and a beautiful French cryptologist are commissioned to decipher a

message left by the curator before his death. The message turns out to reveal the most profound conspiracy in the history of humankind: a cover-up of the true message of Jesus Christ by a secret arm of the Roman Catholic Church called Opus Dei.

Before his death, the curator had evidence that could disprove the deity of Christ. Although (according to the plot) the church tried for centuries to suppress the evidence, great thinkers and artists have planted clues everywhere: in paintings such as the *Mona Lisa* and *Last Supper* by da Vinci, in the architecture of cathedrals, even in Disney cartoons. The book's main claims are these:

• The Roman emperor Constantine conspired to deify Jesus Christ.

• Constantine personally selected the books of the New Testament.

• The Gnostic gospels were banned by men to suppress women.

• Jesus and Mary Magdalene were secretly married and had a child.

• Thousands of secret documents disprove key points of Christianity.

Brown reveals his conspiracy through the book's fictional expert, British royal historian Sir Leigh Teabing. Presented as a wise old scholar, Teabing reveals to cryptologist Sophie Neveu that at the Council of Nicaea in 325 A.D. "many aspects of Christianity were debated and voted upon," including the divinity of Jesus. "Until that moment in history," he says, "Jesus was viewed by His followers as a mortal prophet … a great and powerful man, but a man nonetheless." Neveu is shocked. "Not the Son of God?" she asks.

Teabing explains: "Jesus' establishment as

'the Son of God' was officially proposed and voted on by the Council of Nicaea."

"Hold on. You're saying Jesus' divinity was the result of a vote?"

"A relatively close vote at that," Teabing tells the stunned cryptologist.[2]

In many ways, The Da Vinci Code is the ultimate conspiracy theory. If Brown's assertions are correct, then we have been lied to—by the church, by history, and by the Bible. Perhaps even by those we trust most: our parents or teachers. And it was all for the sake of a power grab.

So, according to Teabing, Jesus was not regarded as God until the Council of Nicaea in 325 A.D., when the real records of Jesus were allegedly banned and destroyed. Thus, according to the theory, the entire foundation of Christianity rests upon a lie.

The Da Vinci Code has sold its story well, drawing comments from readers: "If it were not true it could not have been published!" Another said he would "never set foot in a church again." A reviewer of the book praised it for its "impeccable research."[3] Pretty convincing for a fictional work.

Let's accept for the moment that Teabing's proposal might be true. Why, in that case, would the Council of Nicaea decide to promote Jesus to Godhood?

"It was all about power," Teabing continues. "Christ as Messiah was critical to the functioning of Church and state. Many scholars claim that the early Church literally stole Jesus from His original followers, hijacking His human message, shrouding it in an impenetrable cloak of divinity, and using it to expand their own power."[4]

In many ways, The Da Vinci Code is the ultimate conspiracy theory. If Brown's assertions are correct, then we have been lied to—by the church, by history, and by the Bible. Perhaps even by those we trust most: our parents or teachers. And it was all for the sake of a power grab.

Although The Da Vinci Code is fictional, it does base much of its premise upon actual events (the Council of Nicaea), actual people (Constantine and Arius), and actual documents (the Gnostic gospels). If we are to get to the bottom of the conspiracy, our project must be to address Brown's accusations and separate fact from fiction.

CONSTANTINE AND CHRISTIANITY

In the centuries prior to Constantine's reign over the Roman Empire, Christians had been severely persecuted. But then, while entrenched in warfare, Constantine reported to have seen a bright image of a cross in the sky inscribed with the words "Conquer by this." He marched into battle under the sign of the cross and took control of the empire.

Constantine's apparent conversion to Christianity was a watershed in church history. Rome became a Christian empire. For the first time in nearly 300 years it was relatively safe, and even cool, to be a Christian.

No longer were Christians persecuted for their faith. Constantine then sought to unify his Eastern and Western Empires, which had been badly divided by schisms, sects, and cults, centering mostly around the issue of Jesus Christ's identity.

These are some of the kernels of truth in *The Da Vinci Code*, and kernels of truth are a prerequisite for any successful conspiracy theory. But the book's plot turns Constantine into a conspirator. So let's address a key question raised by Brown's theory: did Constantine invent the Christian doctrine of Jesus' divinity?

HERETICS CONFIRM THE NEW TESTAMENT

The wealthy merchant Marcion (d. c.160 A.D.) didn't like what he thought was the cranky God of the Old Testament, so he removed this God from his version of the Bible. He amputated the entire Old Testament as well as any New Testament books that to him sounded like the Old Testament. We generally know what was in his Bible, and it contained much of what is in ours. What he amputated is harder to discern. The important point is that Marcion's partial list of New Testament books in 135 A.D. affirms their acceptance 200 years prior to the Council of Nicaea.

Tertullian (c.155 or 160–after 220 A.D.), a church father, remarked that there were two ways to butcher scripture. One was Marcion's way—he used a knife to excise from the Scriptures whatever did not conform to his opinion. And according to Tertullian, heretic number two, named Valentinus, showed the other way. Valentinus kept the agreed-upon New Testament books intact but scribbled in his own changes as he saw fit.

If only we had a copy of what was in Valentinus's gospel we would know for sure what Christians nearly two centuries before Constantine and Nicaea regarded as the official New Testament. Oh, wait a minute—we do.

In 1945 a discovery was made in Upper Egypt, near the town of Nag Hammadi. Fifty-two copies of ancient writings, called the Gnostic gospels were found in 13 leather-bound papyrus codices (handwritten books). They were written in Coptic and belonged to a library in a monastery. Suddenly the mystery of these ancient Valentinian documents was unfolded. Among the 52 writings, scholars discovered works many attribute to the leading Gnostic, Valentinus.

One document, the manifesto of the Valentinian school called "The Gospel of Truth," contains themes and passages from Matthew, Luke, John, 10 of Paul's 13 letters, 1 John, and Revelation and likely contained 2 John, Hebrews, and Jude. This is a sizable portion of our New Testament, and it was in place 120 years after Jesus. In spite of Brown's assertion in *The Da Vinci Code* that "eighty gospels" existed, only New Testament Gospels were alluded to by Valentinus.

Thus, even the "outlaws" of Christianity validate the New Testament's wide acceptance well before Constantine convened the bishops at Nicaea.

DEIFYING JESUS

To answer Brown's accusation, we must first determine what Christians in general believed before Constantine ever convened the council at Nicaea.

Christians had been worshiping Jesus as God since the first century. But in the fourth century, a church leader from the east, Arius, launched a campaign to defend God's oneness. He taught that Jesus was a specially created being, higher than the angels, but not God. Athanasius and most church leaders, on the other hand, were convinced that Jesus was God in the flesh.

Constantine wanted to settle the dispute, hoping to bring peace to his empire, uniting the east and west divisions. Thus, in 325 A.D., he convened more than 300 bishops at Nicaea (now part of Turkey) from throughout the Christian world.

The crucial question is, did the early church think Jesus was the Creator or merely a creation—Son of God or son of a carpenter? So, what did the apostles teach about Jesus? From their very first recorded statements, they regarded him as God. About 30 years after Jesus' death and resurrection, Paul wrote the Philippians that Jesus was God in human form (Philippians 2: 6-7, NLT). And John, a close eye-witness, writes of Jesus' divinity in the following passage:

> In the beginning the Word already existed. He was with God, and he was God. He created everything there is. Nothing exists that he didn't make. Life itself was in him….So the Word became human and lived here on earth among us. (John 1: 1-4, 14, NLT)

Papyrus Bodmer II, Gospel of John
Copyright Martin Bodmer Foundation,
Cologny, Switzerland

This illustrated manuscript above contains the very words (in the original Greek) that we just read from John 1 in English, and it is carbon-dated at 175-225 A.D.

We now see that forensic manuscript evidence contradicts *The Da Vinci Code's* claim that Jesus' divinity was a fourth century invention.

But what does history tell us about the Council of Nicaea? Brown asserts in his book, through Teabing, that the majority of bishops at Nicaea overruled Arius's belief that Jesus was a "mortal prophet" and adopted the doctrine of Jesus' divinity by a "relatively close vote." True or false?

In reality, the vote was a landslide: only two of the 318 bishops dissented. Whereas Arius believed that the Father alone was God, and that Jesus was His supreme creation, the council concluded that Jesus and the Father were of the same divine essence.

The Father, the Son, and the Holy Spirit were deemed to be distinct, coexistent, coeternal Persons, but one God. This doctrine of one God in three Persons became known as the Nicene Creed, and is the central core of the Christian Faith. Now, it is true that Arius was persuasive and had consider-

able influence. The landslide vote came after considerable debate. But in the end the council overwhelmingly declared Arius to be a heretic, since his teaching contradicted what the apostles had taught about Jesus' divinity.

History also confirms that Jesus had publicly condoned the worship he received from his disciples. And, as we have seen, Paul and other apostles clearly taught that Jesus is God and is worthy of worship.

From the first days of the Christian church, Jesus was regarded as far more than a mere man, and most of his followers worshiped him as Lord—the Creator of the universe. So, how could Constantine have invented the doctrine of Jesus' divinity if the church had regarded Jesus as God for more than 200 years? *The Da Vinci Code* doesn't address this question.

WHO WAS MARY MAGDALENE?
WAS JESUS MARRIED?
WOULD JESUS BEING SINGLE BE UN-JEWISH?
DO THE SO-CALLED SECRET GNOSTIC GOSPELS HELP US UNDERSTAND JESUS?

New Testament scholar Darrell Bock goes directly to the source of ancient Christian texts to answer the difficult questions raised by Dan Brown's *The Da Vinci Code*. An invaluable resource for separating fact from fiction.

ANSWERS TO THE QUESTIONS
EVERYONE'S ASKING

BREAKING
THE
DA VINCI
CODE

DARRELL L. BOCK, PH.D.

PROFESSOR FRANCIS J. MOLONEY, S.D.B., D.PHIL.

FIRING ON THE CANON

The Da Vinci Code also states that Constantine suppressed all documents about Jesus other than those found in our current New Testament canon (recognized by the church as authentic eyewitness reports of the apostles). It further asserts that the New Testament accounts were altered by Constantine and the bishops to reinvent Jesus. Another key element of *The Da Vinci Code* conspiracy is that the four New Testament Gospels were cherry-picked from a total of "more than 80 gospels," most of which were supposedly suppressed by Constantine.[5]

There are two central issues here, and we need to address both. The first is whether Constantine altered or biased the selection of the New Testament books. The second is whether he barred documents that should have been included in the Bible.

Regarding the first issue, letters and documents written by second century church leaders and heretics alike confirm the wide

Leonardo da Vinci
(1452-1519)

usage of the New Testament books. Nearly 200 years before Constantine convened the Council of Nicaea, the heretic Marcion listed 11 of the 27 New Testament books as being the authentic writings of the apostles.

And about the same time, another heretic, Valentinus, alludes to a wide variety of New Testament themes and passages. Since these two heretics were opponents of the early church leadership, their writings were not controlled by the bishops. Yet, like the early church, they still referred to the same New Testament books we read today. (See page 34, "Heretics Confirm the New Testament")

So, if the New Testament was already widely in use 200 years before Constantine and the Council of Nicaea, how could the emperor have invented or altered it? By that time the church was widespread and encompassed hundreds of thousands if not millions of believers, all of whom were familiar with the New Testament accounts.

In his book *The Da Vinci Deception*, an analysis of *The Da Vinci Code*, Dr. Erwin Lutzer remarks,

> Constantine did not decide which books would be in the canon; indeed, the topic of the canon did not even come up at the Council of Nicaea. By that time the early church was reading a canon of books it had determined was the Word of God two hundred years earlier.[6]

Although the official canon was still years from being finalized, the New Testament of today was deemed authentic more than two centuries before Nicaea.

This brings us to our second issue; why were these mysterious Gnostic gospels destroyed and excluded from the New Testament? In the book, Teabing asserts that the Gnostic writings were eliminated from 50 authorized Bibles commissioned by Constantine at the council. He excitedly tells Neveu:

> Because Constantine upgraded Jesus' status almost four centuries *after* Jesus' death, thousands of documents already existed chronicling His life as a *mortal* man. To rewrite the history books, Constantine knew he would need a bold stroke. From this sprang the most profound moment in Christian history. … Constantine commissioned and financed a new Bible, which omitted those gospels that spoke of Christ's human traits and embellished those gospels that made Him godlike. The earlier gospels were outlawed, gathered up, and burned.[7]

Is Teabing right? Let's take a look to see if we can separate fact from fiction.

SECRET "KNOWERS"

The Gnostic gospels are attributed to a group known as (big surprise here) the Gnostics. Their name comes from the Greek word *gnosis*, meaning "knowledge." These people thought they had secret, special knowledge hidden from ordinary people.

Of the 52 writings, only five are actually listed as gospels. As we shall see, these so-called gospels are markedly different from the New Testament Gospels Matthew, Mark, Luke, and John.

As Christianity spread, the Gnostics mixed some doctrines and elements of Christianity into their beliefs, morphing Gnosticism into a counterfeit Christianity. Perhaps they did it to keep recruitment numbers up and make Jesus a poster child for their cause. However, for their system of thought to fit with Christianity, Jesus needed to be reinvented, stripped of both his humanity and his absolute deity.

In *The Oxford History of Christianity* John McManners wrote of the Gnostics' mixture of Christian and mythical beliefs.

> Gnosticism was (and still is) a theosophy with many ingredients. Occultism and oriental mysticism became fused with astrology, magic. … They collected sayings of Jesus shaped to fit their own interpretation (as in the Gospel of Thomas), and offered their adherents an alternative or rival form of Christianity.[8]

EARLY CRITICS

Contrary to Brown's assertions, it was not Constantine who branded the Gnostic beliefs as heretical; it was the apostles themselves. A mild strain of the philosophy was already growing in the first century just decades after the death of Jesus. The apostles, in their teaching and writings, went to great lengths to condemn these beliefs as being opposed to the truth of Jesus, to whom they were eyewitnesses.

Check out, for example, what the apostle John wrote near the end of the first century:

Who is the great liar? The one who says that Jesus is not the Christ. Such people are antichrists, for they have denied the Father and the Son. (1 John 2:22, NIV).

Following the apostles' teaching, the early church leaders unanimously condemned the Gnostics as a cult. Church father Irenaeus, writing 140 years before the Council of Nicaea, confirmed that the Gnostics were condemned by the church as heretics. He also rejected their "gospels." But, referring to the four New Testament Gospels, he said, "It is not possible that the Gospels can be either more or fewer in number than they are." [9]

Christian theologian Origen wrote this in the early third century, more than a hundred years before Nicaea:

> I know a certain gospel which is called "The Gospel according to Thomas" and a "Gospel according to Matthias," and many others have we read—lest we should in any way be considered ignorant because of those who imagine they possess some knowledge if they are acquainted with these. Nevertheless, among all these we have approved solely what the church has recognized, which is that only four gospels should be accepted.[10]

There we have it in the words of a highly regarded early church leader. The Gnostics were recognized as a non-Christian cult well before the Council of Nicaea. But there's more evidence calling into question claims made in *The Da Vinci Code*.

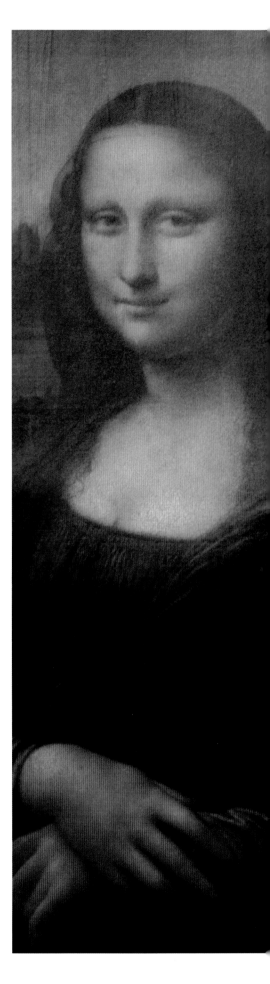

WHO'S SEXIST?

Brown suggests that one of the motives for Constantine's alleged banning of the Gnostic writings was a desire to suppress women in the church. Ironically, it is the Gnostic Gospel of Thomas that demeans women. It concludes (supposedly quoting Peter) with this eye-popping statement: "Let Mary go away from us, because women are not worthy of life."[11] Then Jesus allegedly tells Peter that he will make Mary into a male so that she may enter the kingdom of heaven. Read: women are inferior. With sentiments like that on display, it's difficult to conceive of the Gnostic writings as

> ## "The Gnostic writings were not written by the apostles, but by men in the second century (and later) pretending to use apostolic authority....Today we call this fraud and forgery."
> -Norman Geisler, New Testament scholar

being a battle cry for women's liberation. In stark contrast, the Jesus of the biblical Gospels always treated women with dignity and respect. Revolutionary verses like this one found within the New Testament have been foundational to attempts at raising women's status: "There is no longer Jew or Gentile, slave or free, male or female. For you are all Christians—you are one in Christ Jesus" (Galatians 3:28, NLT).

MYSTERY AUTHORS

When it comes to the Gnostic gospels, just about every book carries the name of a New Testament character: the Gospel of Philip, the Gospel of Peter, the Gospel of Mary, and so on. (Sounds a little like roll call at a parochial school.) These are the books that conspiracy theories like The Da Vinci Code are based upon. But were they even written by their purported authors?

The Gnostic gospels are dated about 110 to 300 years after Christ, and no credible scholar believes any of them could have been written by their namesakes. In James M. Robinson's comprehensive The Nag Hammadi Library, we learn that the Gnostic gospels were written by "largely unrelated and anonymous authors."[12] Dr. Darrell L. Bock, professor of New Testament studies at Dallas Theological Seminary, wrote, "The bulk of this material is a few generations removed from the foundations of the Christian faith, a vital point to remember when assessing the contents."[13]

New Testament scholar Norman Geisler commented on two Gnostic writings, the Gospel of Peter and the Acts of John. (These Gnostic writings are not to be confused with the New Testament books written by John and Peter.) "The Gnostic writings were not written by the apostles, but by men in the second century (and later) pretending to use apostolic authority to advance their own teachings. Today we call this fraud and forgery."[14]

The Gnostic gospels are not historical accounts of Jesus' life but instead are largely esoteric sayings, shrouded in mystery, leaving out historical details such as names, places, and events. This is in striking contrast to the New Testament Gospels, which contain innumerable historical facts about Jesus' life, ministry, and words.

MRS. JESUS

The juiciest part of the Da Vinci conspiracy is the assertion that Jesus and Mary Magdalene had a secret marriage that produced a child, perpetuating his bloodline. Furthermore, Mary Magdalene's womb, carrying Jesus' offspring, is presented in the book as the legendary Holy Grail, a secret closely held by a Catholic organization called the Priory of Sion. Sir Isaac Newton, Botticelli, Victor Hugo, and Leonardo Da Vinci were all cited as members.

Romance. Scandal. Intrigue. Great stuff for a conspiracy theory. But is it true? Let's look at what scholars say.

A Newsweek magazine article, that summarized leading scholars' opinions, concluded that the theory that Jesus and Mary Magdalene were secretly married has no historical basis.[15] The proposal set forth in The Da Vinci Code is built primarily upon one solitary verse in the Gospel of Philip that indicates Jesus and Mary were companions. In the book, Teabing tries to build a case that the word for companion (koinonos) could mean spouse. But Teabing's theory is not accepted by scholars.

There is also a single verse in the Gospel of Philip that says Jesus kissed Mary. Greeting friends with a kiss was common in the first century, and had no sexual connotation. But even if The Da Vinci Code interpretation is correct, there is no other historical document to confirm its theory. And since the Gospel of Philip is a forged document written 150-220 years after Christ by an unknown author, its statement about Jesus isn't historically reliable.

Perhaps the Gnostics felt the New Testament was a bit shy on romance and decided to sauce it up a little. Whatever the reason, this isolated and obscure verse written two centuries after Christ isn't much to base a conspiracy theory upon. Interesting reading perhaps, but definitely not history.

As to the Holy Grail and the Priory of Sion, Brown's fictional account again distorts history. The legendary Holy Grail was supposedly Jesus' cup at his last supper, and had nothing to do with Mary Magdalene. And Leonardo da Vinci never could have known about the Priory of Sion, since it wasn't founded until 1956, 437 years after his death. Again, interesting fiction, but phony history.

THE "SECRET" DOCUMENTS

But what about Teabing's disclosure that "thousands of secret documents" prove that Christianity is a hoax? Could this be true?

If there were such documents, scholars opposed to Christianity would have a field day with them. Fraudulent writings that were rejected by the early church for heretical views are not secret, having been known about for centuries. No surprise there. They have never been considered part of the authentic writings of the apostles.

And if Brown (Teabing) is referring to the apocryphal, or infancy Gospels, that cat is also out of the bag. They are not secret, nor do they disprove Christianity.

New Testament scholar Raymond Brown has said of the Gnostic gospels, "We learn

MYSTERY VERSUS HISTORY

Who would you be more likely to believe—someone who says, "Hey, I've got some secret facts that were mysteriously revealed to me," or someone who says, "I've searched all the evidence and history and here it is for you to make up your mind on"? Keeping that question in mind, consider the following two statements, the first from the Gnostic Gospel of Thomas (c. 110-150 A.D.) and the second from the New Testament's Gospel of Luke (c. 55-70 A.D.).

Gospel of Thomas (c. 110-150 A.D.)
These are the hidden sayings that the living Jesus spoke and Judas Thomas the Twin recorded.[16]

Gospel of Luke (c. 55-70 A.D.)
Many people have written accounts about the events that took place among us. They used as their source material the reports circulating among us from the early disciples and other eyewitnesses of what God has done in fulfillment of his promises. Having carefully investigated all of these accounts from the beginning, I have decided to write a careful summary for you, to reassure you of the truth of all you were taught. (Luke 1:1-4, NLT)

Do you find the open and aboveboard approach of Luke appealing? And do you find the fact that it was written closer to the original events to be in favor of its reliability? If so, that's what the early church thought as well.

New Testament scholar Bruce Metzger revealed why the Gospel of Thomas was not accepted by the early church: "It is not right to say that the Gospel of Thomas was excluded by some fiat on the part of a council: the right way to put it is, the Gospel of Thomas excluded itself! It did not harmonize with other testimony about Jesus that early Christians accepted as trustworthy."[17]

not a single verifiable new fact about the historical Jesus' ministry, and only a few new sayings that might possibly have been his."[18]

Unlike the Gnostic gospels, whose authors are unknown and who were not eyewit-nesses, the New Testament we have today has passed numerous tests for authenticity (see "Jesus.doc" page 42). The contrast is devastating to those pushing conspiracy theories. New Testament historian F. F. Bruce wrote, "There is no body of ancient literature in the world which enjoys such a wealth of good textual attestation as the New Testament."[19]

HISTORY'S VERDICT

So, what are we to conclude regarding the various conspiracy theories about Jesus Christ? Karen King, professor of ecclesiastical history at Harvard, has written several books on the Gnostic gospels, including *The Gospel of Mary of Magdala* and *What Is Gnosticism?* King, though a strong advocate of Gnostic teaching, concluded, "These notions about the conspiracy theory...are all very marginal ideas that have no historical basis."[20]

In spite of the lack of historical evidence, conspiracy theories will still sell millions of books and set box office records. Scholars in related fields, some Christians and some with no faith at all, have disputed the claims of *The Da Vinci Code*. However, the easily swayed will still wonder, *Could there be something to it after all?*

Award-winning television journalist Frank Sesno asked a panel of historical scholars about the fascination people have with conspiracy theories. Professor Stanley Kutler from the University of Wisconsin replied, "We all love mysteries – but we love conspiracies more." [21]

So, if you want to read a great conspiracy theory about Jesus, Dan Brown's novel, *The Da Vinci Code*, may be just the ticket for you. But if you want to read the true accounts of Jesus Christ, then Matthew, Mark, Luke, and John will get you back to what the eyewitnesses saw, heard, and wrote. Who would you rather believe?

"These notions about the conspiracy theory...are all very marginal ideas that have no historical basis."
-Karen King

ENDNOTES

[1] Dan Brown, *The Da Vinci Code* (New York: Doubleday, 2003), 234.

[2] Brown, 233.

[3] Quoted in Erwin Lutzer, *The Da Vinci Deception* (Wheaton, IL: Tyndale, 2004), xix.

[4] Brown, 233.

[5] Brown, 231.

[6] Lutzer, 71.

[7] Brown, 234.

[8] John McManners, ed., *The Oxford History of Christianity* (New York: Oxford University Press, 2002), 28.

[9] Quoted in Darrell L. Bock, *Breaking the Da Vinci Code* (Nashville: Nelson, 2004), 114.

[10] Quoted in Bock, 119-120.

[11] Quoted in James M. Robinson, ed., *The Nag Hammadi Library: The Definitive Translation of the Gnostic Scriptures* (HarperCollins, 1990), 138.

[12] Ibid., 13.

[13] Bock, 64.

[14] Norman Geisler and Ron Brooks, *When Skeptics Ask* (Grand Rapids, MI: Baker, 1998), 156.

[15] Barbara Kantrowitz and Anne Underwood, "Decoding 'The Da Vinci Code,' " *Newsweek*, December 8, 2003, 54.

[16] Quoted in Robinson, 126.

[17] Quoted in Lee Strobel, *The Case for Christ* (Grand Rapids, MI: Zondervan. 1998), 68.

[18] Quoted in Lutzer, 32.

[19] Quoted in Josh McDowell, *The New Evidence that Demands a Verdict* (San Bernardino, CA: Here's Life, 1999, 37.

[20] Quoted in Linda Kulman and Jay Tolson, "Jesus in America," *U. S. News & World Report*, December 22, 2003, 2.

[21] Stanley Kutler, interview with Frank Sesno, "The Guilty Men: An Historical Review," *History Channel*, April 6, 2004.

THE DA VINCI CODE AND THE TRUTH

DA VINCI CODE THEORY: Jesus had a secret marriage with Mary Magdalene that produced a royal bloodline.

TRUTH: This fictional account is primarily based upon one solitary verse in the Gnostic Gospel of Philip. However, scholars believe the correct interpretation of the verse simply means that Jesus and Mary were companions. Since the Gospel of Philip is a forged document written 150-220 years after Christ by an unknown author, its statement about Jesus couldn't be an eyewitness account. No serious scholar contends that Jesus and Mary were married, let alone had a child.

DA VINCI CODE THEORY: Jesus' divinity was invented by Constantine and church bishops at the Council of Nicaea in 325 A. D.

TRUTH: Ancient New Testament manuscripts such as the Gospel of John clearly speak of Jesus' divinity at least 100 years before the Council of Nicaea. Furthermore, letters from early church fathers, and other historical documents confirm that Christians worshipped Jesus as God at least 200 years before Constantine convened the bishops.

DA VINCI CODE THEORY: Constantine personally selected the books we have in the New Testament. Thus the accounts of Jesus we read today are forgeries written by unknown writers.

TRUTH: Evidence is irrefutable that the books in today's New Testament were widely believed to be the words of the apostles at least 200 years prior to the Council of Nicaea. Constantine did authorize 50 new Bibles to be written, but the books they contained had already existed for at least two centuries.

DA VINCI CODE THEORY: The Gnostic Gospels were destroyed by Constantine as a power play, and as a way to suppress women. These 52 Gospels, which include The Gospel of Thomas, The Gospel of Mary, and The Gospel of Philip, give us the real history of Jesus that Constantine and the church leaders had hijacked.

TRUTH: The Gnostic writings date 110 to 300 years after Christ, and could not have been written by Jesus' followers. In effect they are forgeries with unknown authors. The Gnostics were a cult that was condemned by the apostles and early church fathers well before Constantine. Their passages on Jesus (other than New Testament verses they quote) are highly suspect due to their late dating, unknown authors, and lack of historical detail. Even though many feminists embrace them, several of their passages demean women.

DA VINCI CODE THEORY: Thousands of secret documents disprove Christianity.

TRUTH: No credible document exists that in any way disproves Christianity. On the contrary, there is overwhelming evidence that substantiates the New Testament (also see article 4). This includes documents from secular historians, church historians, heretics, early church leaders, and archaeological evidence. If such secret documents really did exist, every opponent of Christianity would be screaming for them to be made public.

Jesus.doc
Is the New Testament reliable?

In July 2000 ABC News anchor Peter Jennings was in Israel broadcasting a television special on Jesus Christ. His program, "The Search for Jesus," explored the question of whether the Jesus of the New Testament was historically accurate. Jennings featured opinions on the Gospel accounts from DePaul professor John Dominic Crossan, three of Crossan's colleagues from the Jesus Seminar, and two other Bible scholars. [1]

Some of the comments were stunning. There on national TV Dr. Crossan not only cast doubt on more than 80 percent of Jesus' sayings but also denied Jesus' claims to divinity, his miracles, and his resurrection. Jennings clearly was intrigued by the image of Jesus presented by Crossan.

Searching for true Bible history is always news, which is why every year *Time* and *Newsweek* go on a cover story quest for Mary, Jesus, Moses, or Abraham. Or—who knows?—maybe this year it will be "Bob: The Untold Story of the Missing 13th Disciple."

But Jennings's report did focus on one issue that ought to be given some serious thought. Crossan implied that the original accounts of Jesus were embellished by oral tradition and were not written down until after the apostles were dead. Thus they are largely unreliable and fail to give us an accurate picture of the real Jesus. How are we to know if this is really true?

So what does the evidence show? When were the original documents of the New Testament written? And who wrote them?

LOST IN TRANSLATION?

So, what does the evidence show? We begin with two simple questions: When were the original documents of the New Testament written? And who wrote them?

The importance of these questions should be obvious. If the accounts of Jesus were written after the eyewitnesses were dead, no one could verify their accuracy. But if the New Testament accounts were written while the original apostles were still alive, then their authenticity could be established. Peter could say of a forgery in his name, "Hey, I didn't write that." And Matthew, Mark, Luke, or John could respond to questions or challenges aimed at their accounts of Jesus.

The New Testament writers claimed to be rendering eyewitness accounts of Jesus. The apostle Peter stated it this way in one letter: "We were not making up clever stories when we told you about the power of our Lord Jesus Christ and his coming again. We have seen his majestic splendor with our own eyes" (2 Peter 1:16, NLT).

ANCIENT GREEK DOCUMENT COMPARISON (PARTIAL & COMPLETE MANUSCRIPTS)[3]

AUTHOR	BOOK	WRITTEN	EARLIEST COPIES	GAP FROM ORIGINAL	NUMBER OF COPIES
Homer	*Iliad*	800 B.C.	c.400 b.c.	400 yrs.	643
Herodotus	*History*	480–425 B.C.	c.900 a.d.	1,350 yrs.	8
Thucydides	*History*	460–400 B.C.	c.900 a.d.	1,300 yrs.	8
Plato		400 B.C.	c.900 a.d.	1,300 yrs.	7
Demosthenes		300 B.C.	c.1100 a.d.	1,400 yrs.	200
Caesar	*Gallic Wars*	100–44 B.C.	c.900 a.d.	1,000 yrs.	10
Livy	*History of Rome*	59 B.C.–A.D.17	part—4th cent.	400 yrs.	1 partial
			most—10th cent.	1,000 yrs.	19 copies
Tacitus	*Annals*	A.D. 100	c.1100 a.d.	1,000 yrs.	20
Pliny Secundus	*Natural History*	A.D. 61–113	c.850 a.d.	750 yrs.	7
New Testament		A.D. 50–100	fragment—c.114	+ 50 yrs.	5,366
			books—c.200	100 yrs.	
			most—c.250	150 yrs.	
			complete—c.325	225 yrs.	

A major part of the New Testament is the apostle Paul's 13 letters to young churches and individuals. Paul's letters, dated between the mid 40s and the mid 60s (12 to 33 years after Christ), constitute the earliest witnesses to Jesus' life and teaching.

Will Durant wrote of the historical importance of Paul's letters, "The Christian evidence for Christ begins with the letters ascribed to Saint Paul. ... No one has questioned the existence of Paul, or his repeated meetings with Peter, James, and John; and Paul enviously admits that these men had known Christ in the flesh."[2]

BUT IS IT TRUE?

In books, magazines, and TV documentaries, the Jesus Seminar suggests the Gospels were written as late as 130 A.D. to 150 A.D. by unknown authors. If those later dates are correct, there would be a gap of approximately 100 years from Christ's death (scholars put Jesus' death between 30 and 33) A.D. And since all the eyewitnesses would have been dead, the Gospels could only have been written by unknown, fraudulent authors.

So, what evidence do we have concerning when the Gospel accounts of Jesus were really written? The consensus of most scholars is that the Gospels were written by the apostles during the first century. They cite several reasons that we will review later in this article.

For now, however, note that three primary forms of evidence appear to build a solid case for their conclusions:

- early documents from heretics such as Marcion and the school of Valentinus citing New Testament books, themes, and passages (see "Mona Lisa's Smirk")

- numerous writings of early Christian sources, such as Clement of Rome, Ignatius, and Polycarp

- discovered copies of Gospel fragments carbon-dated as early as 117 A.D.

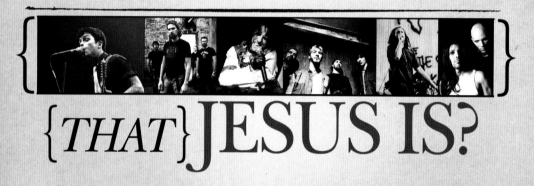
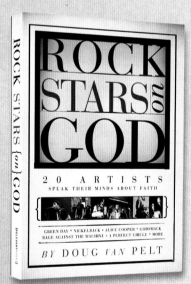

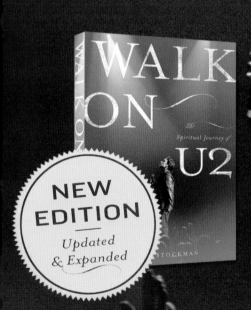

Biblical archaeologist William Albright concluded on the basis of his research that all the New Testament books were written while most of the apostles were still alive. He wrote, "We can already say emphatically that there is no longer any solid basis for dating any book after about 80 A.D., two full generations before the date of between 130 A.D. and 150 A.D. given by the more radical New Testament critics of today."[4] Elsewhere Albright put the writing of the entire New Testament at "very probably sometime between about 50 A.D. and 75 A.D."[5]

The notoriously skeptical scholar John A. T. Robinson dates the New Testament earlier than even most conservative scholars. In *Redating the New Testament* Robinson asserts that most of the New Testament was written between 40 A.D. and 65 A.D. That puts its writing as early as seven years after Christ lived.[6] If that is true, any historical errors would have been immediately exposed by both eyewitnesses and the enemies of Christianity.

So let's look at the trail of clues that takes us from the original documents to our New Testament copies today.

WHO NEEDS KINKO'S?

The original writings of the apostles were revered. Churches studied them, shared them, carefully preserved them and stored them away like buried treasure.

But, alas, Roman confiscations, the passage of 2,000 years, and the second law of thermodynamics have taken their toll. So, today, what do we have of those original

writings? Nothing. The original manuscripts are all gone (though each week Bible scholars, no doubt, tune in to *Antiques Roadshow* hoping one might emerge).

Yet the New Testament is not alone in this fate; no other comparable document from ancient history exists today either. Historians aren't troubled by the lack of original manuscripts if they have reliable copies to examine. But are there ancient copies of the New Testament available, and if so, are they faithful to the originals?

As the number of churches multiplied, hundreds of copies were carefully made under the supervision of church leaders. Every letter was meticulously penned in ink on parchment or papyrus. And so, today, scholars can study the surviving copies (and the copies of copies, and the copies of copies of copies—you get it), to determine authenticity and arrive at a very close approximation of the original documents.

In fact, scholars studying ancient literature have devised the science of textual criticism to examine documents such as *The Odyssey*, comparing them with other ancient documents to determine their accuracy. More recently, military historian Charles Sanders augmented textual criticism by devising a three-part test that looks at not only the faithfulness of the copy but also the credibility of the authors. His tests are these:

1. The bibliographical test
2. The internal evidence test
3. The external evidence test[7]

Let's see what happens when we apply these tests to the early New Testament manuscripts.

"Luke is a historian of the first rank.... This author should be placed along with the very greatest historians...Luke's history is unsurpassed in trustworthiness."

Sir William Ramsey, Archaeologist

BIBLIOGRAPHICAL TEST

This test compares a document with other ancient history from the same period. It asks:

- How many copies of the original document are in existence?
- How large of a time gap is there between the original writings and the earliest copies?
- How well does a document compare with other ancient history?

Imagine if we had only two or three copies of the original New Testament manuscripts. The sampling would be so small that we couldn't possibly verify accuracy.

On the other hand, if we had hundreds or even thousands, we could easily weed out the errors of poorly transmitted documents.

So, how well does the New Testament compare with other ancient writings with regard to both the number of copies and the time gap from the originals? More than 5,000 manuscripts of the New Testament exist today in the original Greek language. When counting translations into other languages, the number is a staggering 24,000—dating from the 2ND to 4TH centuries. Compare that with the second-best-document-ed ancient historical manuscript, Homer's *Iliad*, with 643 copies.[8] And remember that most ancient historical works have far fewer existing manuscripts than that one does (usually fewer than 10). New Testament scholar Bruce Metzger remarked, "In contrast with these figures [of other ancient manuscripts], the textual critic of the New Testament is embarrassed by the wealth of his material."[9]

"The wealth of manuscripts, and above all the narrow interval of time between the writing and the earliest extant copies makes it [the New Testament] by far the best attested text of any ancient writing of the world."
John A. T. Robinson, critical scholar

Fragment of St. John's Gospel: Recto (p52)
Reproduced by courtesy of the Director & Librarian, The John Rylands University Library,

Papyrus Bodmer XV, Gospel of John c. 175-225 A. D.
Coyright Martin Bodmer Foundation, Cologny, Switzerland

TIME GAP

Not only is the number of manuscripts significant, but so is the time gap between when the original was written and the date of the copy. Over the course of a thousand years of copying, there's no telling what a text could evolve into—But over a hundred years, that's a different story.

German critic Ferdinand Christian Baur (1792–1860) once contended that John's Gospel was not written until about 160 A.D.; therefore, it could not have been written by John. This, if true, would have not only undermined John's writings but cast suspicion on the entire New Testament as well. But then, when a cache of New Testament papyri fragments were discovered in Egypt, among them was a fragment of the Gospel of John (specifically, P52: John 18:31-33) dated to roughly 25 years after John wrote the original.

Metzger explained, "Just as Robinson Crusoe, seeing but a single footprint in the sand, concluded that another human being, with two feet, was present on the island with him, so P52 [the label of the fragment]

proves the existence and use of the Fourth Gospel during the first half of the second century in a provincial town along the Nile far removed from its traditional place of composition (Ephesus in Asia Minor)."[10] Find after find, archeology has unearthed copies of major portions of the New Testament dated to within 150 years of the originals.[11]

Most other ancient documents have time gaps of from 400 to 1,400 years. For example, Aristotle's *Poetics* was written about 343 B.C., yet the earliest copy is dated 1100 A.D., with only five copies in existence. And yet no one is going in search of the historical Plato, claiming he was actually a fireman and not a philosopher.

In fact, there is a nearly complete copy of the Bible called, Codex Vaticanus, that was written only about 250 to 300 years after the apostles' original writing. The oldest known complete copy of the New Testament in ancient uncial script is named, Codex Sinaiticus, now housed at the British Museum.

Like Codex Vaticanus, it is dated from the

fourth century. Vaticanus and Sinaiticus, going back to early in Christian history, are like other early biblical manuscripts in that they differ minimally from each other and give us a very good picture of what the original documents must have said.

Even critical scholar John A. T. Robinson has admitted, "The wealth of manuscripts, and above all the narrow interval of time between the writing and the earliest extant copies, make it by far the best attested text of any ancient writing in the world."[12] Professor of law John Warwick Montgomery affirmed, "To be skeptical of the resultant text of the New Testament books is to allow all of classical antiquity to slip into obscurity, for no documents of the ancient period are as well attested bibliographically as the New Testament."[13]

The point is this: If the New Testament records were made and circulated so closely to the actual events, their portrayal of Jesus is most likely accurate. But external evidence is not the only way to answer the question of reliability; scholars also use internal evidence to answer this question.

THE DISCOVERY OF CODEX SINAITICUS

In 1844 the German scholar Constantine Tischendorf was searching for New Testament manuscripts. By accident, he noticed a basket filled with old pages in the library of the monastery of St. Catherine at Mount Sinai. The German scholar was both elated and shocked. He had never seen Greek manuscripts that old. Tischendorf asked the librarian about them and was horrified to learn that the pages had been discarded to be used as fuel. Two basketloads of such papers had already been burned!

Tischendorf's enthusiasm made the monks wary, and they would not show him any more manuscripts. However, they did allow Tischendorf to take the 43 pages he had discovered.

Fifteen years later, Tischendorf returned to the Sinai monastery, this time with help from the Russian Tsar Alexander II. Once he was there, a monk took Tischendorf to his room and pulled down a cloth-wrapped manuscript that had been stored on a shelf with cups and dishes. Tischendorf immediately recognized the valuable remaining portions of the manuscripts he had seen earlier.

The monastery agreed to present the manuscript to the tsar of Russia as protector of the Greek Church. In 1933 the Soviet Union sold the manuscript to the British Museum for £100,000.

Codex Sinaiticus is one of the earliest complete manuscripts of the New Testament we have, and it is among the most important. Some speculate that it is one of the 50 Bibles the emperor Constantine commissioned Eusebius to prepare in the early fourth century. Codex Sinaiticus has been of enormous help to scholars in verifying the accuracy of the New Testament.

"To be skeptical of the resultant text of the New Testament books is to allow all of classical antiquity to slip into obscurity, for no documents of the ancient period are as well attested bibliographically as the New Testament."

John Warwick Montgomery
Professor of Law

INTERNAL EVIDENCE TEST

Like good detectives, historians verify reliability by looking at internal clues. Such clues reveal motives of the authors and their willingness to disclose details and other features that could be verified. The key internal clues these scholars use to test for reliability are the following:

- consistency of eyewitness reports
- details of names, places, and events
- letters to individuals or small groups
- features embarrassing to the authors
- the presence of irrelevant or counter-productive material
- lack of relevant material[14]

These are but a few examples of how internal evidence leads either toward or away from the conclusion that a document is historically reliable. We'll look briefly at the internal evidence for the historicity of the New Testament.

WHAT'S IN THERE?

Several aspects of the New Testament help us determine its reliability based on its own content and qualities.

Consistency. Phony documents either leave out eyewitness reports or are inconsistent. So outright contradiction among the Gospels would prove that they contain errors. But at the same time, if each Gospel said exactly the same thing, it would raise suspicions of collusion. It would be like co-conspirators trying to agree on every detail of their scheme. Too much consistency is as doubtful as too little.

Eyewitnesses to a crime or an accident generally get the big events right but see it from different perspectives. For example, everyone agrees that President John Kennedy was assassinated, but eyewitness reports differ somewhat on the details of how many shots were fired, and from which direction they came.

Likewise, the four Gospels describe the events of Jesus' life from different perspectives. Yet, regardless of these perspectives, Bible scholars are amazed at the consistency of their accounts and the clear picture of Jesus and his teaching they put together with their complementary reports.

Details. Historians love details in a document because they make it easy to verify reliability. Paul's letters are filled with details. And the Gospels abound with them. For example, both Luke's Gospel and his Book of Acts were written to a nobleman named Theophilus, who was undoubtedly a well-known individual at the time.

If these writings had been mere inventions of the apostles, phony names, places, and events would have quickly been spotted by

PONTIUS PILATE INSCRIPTION

their enemies, the Jewish and Roman leaders. This would have become the Watergate of the first century. Yet many of the New Testament details have been proved true by independent verification. Classical historian Colin Hemer, for example, "identifies 84 facts in the last 16 chapters of Acts that have been confirmed by Archaeological research."[15]

In the previous few centuries, skeptical Bible scholars attacked both Luke's authorship and its dating, asserting that it was written in the second century by an unknown author. Archaeologist Sir William Ramsey was convinced they were right, and he began to investigate. After extensive research, the archaeologist reversed his opinion. Ramsey conceded, "Luke is a historian of the first rank. … This author should be placed along with the very greatest historians. … Luke's history is unsurpassed in respect of its trustworthiness."[16]

Acts chronicles Paul's missionary voyages, listing places he visited, people he saw, messages he delivered, and persecution he suffered. Could all these details have been faked? Roman historian A. N. Sherwin-White wrote, "For Acts the confirmation of historicity is overwhelming. … Any attempt to reject its basic historicity must now appear absurd. Roman historians have long taken it for granted."[17]

From the Gospel accounts to Paul's letters, the New Testament authors openly described details, even citing the names of individuals who were alive at the time. Historians have verified at least thirty of these names.[18]

Letters to small groups. Most forged texts are from documents both general and public in nature, like this magazine article (no doubt countless forgeries are already circulating on the black market). Historical expert Louis Gottschalk notes that personal letters intended for small audiences have a high probability of being reliable.[19] Which category do the New Testament documents fall into?

Well, some of them were clearly intended to be circulated widely. Yet large portions of the New Testament consist of personal letters written to small groups and individuals. These documents, at least, would not be considered prime candidates for falsification.

Embarrassing features. Most writers don't want to publicly embarrass themselves. Historians have therefore observed that documents containing embarrassing revelations about the authors are generally to be trusted. What did the New Testament authors say about themselves?

If these [New Testament] writings had been mere inventions of the apostles…. This would have become the Watergate of the first century.

Surprisingly, the authors of the New Testament presented themselves as all too frequently dimwitted, cowardly, and faithless. For example, consider Peter's threefold denial of Jesus or the disciples' arguments over which of them was the greatest—both stories recorded in the Gospels. As respect for the apostles was crucial in the early church, inclusion of this kind of material doesn't make sense unless the apostles were reporting truthfully.[20]

In *The Story of Civilization*, Will Durant wrote about the apostles, "These men were hardly of the type that one would have chosen to remold the world. The Gospels realistically differentiate their characters, and honestly expose their faults."[21]

Counterproductive or irrelevant material. The Gospels tell us that the empty tomb of Jesus was discovered by a woman, even though in Israel the testimony of women was considered to be virtually worthless and was not even admissible in court. Jesus' mother and family are recorded as stating their belief that he had lost his mind. Some of Jesus' final words on the cross are said to have been "My God, my God, why have you forsaken me?" And so goes the list of incidents recorded in the New Testament that are counterproductive if the intent of the author were anything but the accurate transmission of the life and teachings of Jesus Christ.

Lack of relevant material. It is ironic (or perhaps logical) that few of the major issues facing the first-century church—the Gentile mission, spiritual gifts, baptism, leadership—were addressed directly in the recorded words of Jesus. If his follow-ers were simply generating the material to encourage the growing church, it is inexplicable why they would not have made up instructions from Jesus on these issues. In one case, the apostle Paul flatly stated about a certain subject, "On this we have no teaching from the Lord."

EXTERNAL EVIDENCE TEST

The third and final measure of a document's reliability is the external evidence test, which asks, "Do historical records outside the New Testament confirm its reliability?" So, what did non-Christian historians say about Jesus Christ?

"Overall, at least seventeen non-Christian writings record more than fifty details concerning the life, teachings, death, and resurrection of Jesus, plus details concerning the early church."[22] This is astounding, considering the lack of other history we possess from this time period. Jesus is mentioned by more sources than the conquests of Caesar during this same period. It is even more astounding since these confirmations of New Testament details date from 20 to 150 years after Christ, "quite early by the standards of ancient historiography."[23]

The reliability of the New Testament is further substantiated by over 36,000 extra-biblical Christian documents (quotes from church leaders of the first three centuries) dating as early as ten years after the last writing of the New Testament.[24] If all the copies of the New Testament were lost, you could reproduce it from these other letters and documents with the exception of a few verses.[25]

Boston University professor emeritus Howard Clark Kee concludes, "The result of the examination of the sources outside the New Testament that bear … on our knowledge of Jesus is to confirm his historical existence, his unusual powers, the devotion of his followers, the continued existence of the movement after his death … and the penetration of Christianity … in Rome itself by the later first century."[26]

The external evidence test thus builds on the evidence provided by other tests. In spite of the conjecture of a few radical skeptics, the New Testament portrait of the real Jesus Christ is virtually smudgeproof. Although there are a few dissenters such as the Jesus Seminar, the consensus of experts, regardless of their religious beliefs, confirms that the New Testament we read today faithfully represents both the words and events of Jesus' life.

Clark Pinnock, professor of interpretations at McMaster Divinity College, summed it up well when he said, "There exists no document from the ancient world witnessed by so excellent a set of textual and historical testimonies. … An honest [person] cannot dismiss a source of this kind. Skepticism regarding the historical credentials of Christianity is based upon an irrational basis."[27]

ENDNOTES

[1] According to jesusseminar.org, "The Jesus Seminar was organized under the auspices of the Westar Institute to renew the quest of the historical Jesus. At the close of debate on each agenda item, Fellows of the Seminar vote, using colored beads to indicate the degree of authenticity of Jesus' words or deeds."

[2] Will Durant, *Caesar and Christ*, vol. 3 of The Story of Civilization (New York: Simon & Schuster, 1972), 555.

[3] Josh McDowell, *The New Evidence That Demands A Verdict* (Nashville: Thomas Nelson Publishers, 1999), 38.

[4] William F. Albright, *Recent Discoveries in Biblical Lands* (New York: Funk & Wagnalls, 1955), 136.

[5] William F. Albright, "Toward a More Conservative View," *Christianity Today*, January 18, 1993, 3.

[6] John A. T. Robinson, *Redating the New Testament*, quoted in Norman L. Geisler and Frank Turek, *I Don't Have Enough Faith to Be an Atheist* (Wheaton, IL: Crossway, 2004), 243.

[7] McDowell, 33-68.

[8] McDowell, 34.

[9] Bruce M. Metzger, *The Text of the New Testament* (New York: Oxford University Press, 1992), 34.

[10] Metzger, 39.

[11] Metzger, 36-41.

[12] John A. T. Robinson, *Can We Trust the New Testament?* (Grand Rapids: Eerdmans, 1977), 36.

[13] Quoted in McDowell, 36.

[14] J. P. Moreland, *Scaling the Secular City* (Grand Rapids: Baker, 2000), 134-157.

[15] Quoted in Geisler and Turek, 256.

[16] Quoted in McDowell, 61.

[17] Quoted in McDowell, 64.

[18] Geisler and Turek, 269.

[19] J. P. Moreland, 136-137.

[20] Geisler and Turek, 276.

[21] Durant, 563.

[22] Gary R. Habermas, "Why I Believe the New Testament is Historically Reliable," *Why I am a Christian*, eds Norman L. Geisler & Paul K. Hoffman (Grand Rapids, MI: Baker, 2001), 150.

[23] Ibid.

[24] Ibid.

[25] Metzger, 86.

[26] Quoted in McDowell, 135.

[27] Quoted in Josh McDowell, *The Resurrection Factor* (San Bernardino, CA: Here's Life Publishers, 1981), 9.

w as the **MESS IAH'S** IDENTITY ENCRYPTED

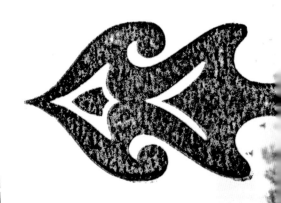

WITHIN

ANCIENT Hebrew

PROPHECY?

THE path

LAID BY

PROPHETS BY

Ferdinand Waldo Demara Jr. was called, the great imposter. Demara held phony identities of psychologist, university lecturer, college department head, school teacher, and prison warden. He even performed surgeries, as a bogus doctor.

Some argue that Frank Abagnale was an even greater imposter. Between the ages of 16 and 21, Abagnale was one of the world's most successful con artists. He cashed $2.5 million in fraudulent checks in all 50 states and 26 foreign countries. He also successfully passed himself off as an airline pilot, an attorney, a college professor, and a pediatrician before being apprehended by the French police.

If this story sounds familiar to you, it's probably because you watched the 2002 movie *Catch Me If You Can*, in which Abagnale was played by Leonardo DiCaprio (who passed himself off as an actor in *Titanic*).

What would it take to top Abagnale's performance as a con man? Well, if Jesus Christ wasn't the Messiah he claimed to be, there would be no contest. We're not talking about conning thousands, as in the case of Abagnale. If Jesus Christ was an imposter, his con job has deluded billions of people and changed the course of 2,000 years of history.

So, could Jesus have been a fake Messiah, fooling even the most noteworthy religious scholars? Is it possible he was groomed by his parents or undisclosed mentors to become the long-promised king that Israel had been looking for?

In fact, if Jesus was an imposter, he would not be the first person in the history of Israel to have lied about being the Messiah. Through the centuries prior to Christ's birth, and afterward as well, many self-proclaimed messiahs arose, only to be shown to be cons or lunatics.

Ancient Hebrew prophecies had clearly predicted the reign of a future king who would bring peace to Israel and be their Savior. A sense of expectancy filled the land and captivated Jewish hopes and aspirations. In such an atmosphere as Israel's, could not someone less qualified have been pressed into, or conformed himself to fit, the mold of Messiah? The answer to that question hangs on the Old Testament prophecies pointing to the Messiah.

GOD'S MOUTHPIECES

According to the Scriptures, the God of the Hebrews spoke to his people through prophets, men and women who were especially attuned to God and who may or may not have been a part of the religious establishment. Some of the prophets' messages were for the present; others, for the future. Either way, their role was to proclaim God's declarations and disclosures to the people.

In general, being a prophet ranked up there with working at a meatpacking plant among the world's most hazardous occupations. Even when they were telling the truth, prophets might be killed or thrown into prison by people who didn't like what they were saying. (Some kings hated hearing bad news.) According to historical accounts, the prophet Isaiah was sawn in half.

If Jesus Christ was an imposter, his con job has deluded billions of people and changed the course of 2,000 years of history.

So consider a prophet's dilemma: death if he was proved wrong and the possibility of death if he was right. No true prophet wanted to offend God, and just as few wanted to be sawn in half. Thus most prophets waited until they were absolutely convinced that God had spoken, or else they kept their mouths shut. Kings began to shudder at their words. A true prophet's messages were never wrong.

Now here's a question: how would the accuracy of these biblical prophets match up with today's psychics?

PROPHETS AS PSYCHICS?

To consider whether modern psychics' accuracy approaches that of biblical prophets, let's take Jean Dixon as a case study. This American psychic seemed to have a special ability to foretell events. But upon analysis her reputation seems unwarranted.

For instance, Dixon had a vision that on February 5, 1962, a child was born in the Middle East who would transform the world by the year 2000. This special man would create a one-world religion and bring lasting world peace. She saw a cross growing above this man until it covered the whole earth. According to Dixon, this child would be a descendant of the ancient Egyptian Queen Nefertiti. [1]

Where is this guy? Have you seen him? And how about that lasting world peace—it's nice, huh?

In fact, an exhaustive search of her prediction yields two indisputable facts. Her rate of accuracy is equivalent to those guessing the future, and her most publicized fulfillments were prophecies so intentionally vague as any number of events could have been hailed as fulfillments.

Even the widely publicized prophecies of Nostradamus have frequently been proved wrong in spite of his vague oracles, which are difficult to disprove. [2] For example, here is one of the predictions of Nostradamus:

> Takes the Goddess of the Moon, for
> his Day & Movement:
> A frantic wanderer and witness of
> Gods Law,
> In awakening the worlds great
> regions to Gods will (Ones Will). [3]

This is said to be about the death of Princess Diana. (You were probably thinking Margaret Thatcher.) Prophecies like this are as nebulous as seeing images in clouds. Yet some insist this is evidence of a Nostradamus prophecy fulfilled. Highly suspect, but difficult to disprove.

And this is generally the track record of psychics. When "The People's Almanac" researched the predictions of 25 top psychics, 92 percent of the predictions had proved wrong. The other 8 percent were questionable and could be explained by chance or general knowledge of circumstances. [4] In other experiments with the world's foremost psychics, their rate of accuracy has been shown to hover around 11 percent, which might not be a bad average except for the fact that people making random guesses about the future score at the same percentile. This doesn't disprove all future telling, but it certainly explains why psychics aren't winning the lottery.

The difference between psychics and prophets seems to be more one of kind than one of degree. Prophets made specific declarations about future events in relation to God's unfurling plan—and did it with unwavering accuracy. Psychics are more mercenary, providing vague sketches of the future to a market willing to pay for their services. They offer sensational information, but with a flawed track record.

According to the Hebrew requirements that a prophecy must have a 100 percent rate of accuracy, the true Messiah of Israel must fulfill them all or else he is not the Messiah.

religious PROPHECY IN

PERSPECTIVE

Prophecy can be rather mystical, metaphysical, and—for lack of a better word—creepy. It conjures up images of séances and other worlds. In *Star Wars* there is the foretelling of one who would bring balance to the Force. The Lord of the Rings movies weave their imaginary themes around scenes of prophetic utterances. But such is the world of imagination.

Regarding the real world, it has been said that if a person knew just one minute of the future he could rule the world. Think about it. One minute of knowing every hand dealt at the Trump Casino. You'd become the richest person in the world and Donald would become a postal worker.

But in the world of religion, prophecy serves an important function. It becomes one sure way to know if someone is speaking from God or if he is not, for only an omniscient God could exhaustively know the future. And on this point the prophecy in the Old Testament stands as unique, for most of the renowned holy books from other religions are devoid of predictive prophecy. For example, while the Book of Mormon and the Hindu Veda claim divine inspiration, there is really no means to corroborate their claims; you're simply left with "Yeah, that sounds like something God might say."

Bible scholar Wilbur Smith compared the prophecies of the Bible with other historical books, stating that the Bible "is the only volume ever produced by man, or a group of men, in which is to be found a large body of prophecies relating to individual nations, to Israel, to all the peoples of the earth, to certain cities, and to the coming one who was to be the Messiah."[5] Thus the Bible lays out its claim for inspiration in such a way that it can be either substantiated or disproved.

And if you put this degree of accuracy into everyday perspective, you can see how astounding it is. For example, it would have been miraculous if in 1910 you had predicted that a man named George Bush

would win the 2000 election. But imagine if you had included some of these details in your prediction:

- The candidate with the most total votes would lose the election.
- All major TV networks would announce the winner and then reverse themselves.
- One state (Florida) would swing the election.
- The U.S. Supreme Court would ultimately determine the winner.

Had such occurred, there would be churches named after you and dashboard statuettes bearing your likeness. But you didn't, so there aren't. As difficult (or impossible) as it would have been in 1910 to have accurately predicted this precise sequence of events, the odds are incredibly more difficult for Jesus, or any one person, to have fulfilled all the Hebrew prophecies for the Messiah. Contained within the Old Testament, written hundreds of years before the birth of Jesus, are 61 specific prophecies and nearly 300 references about the Messiah.[6]

According to the Hebrew requirement that a prophecy must have a 100 percent rate of accuracy, the true Messiah of Israel must

fulfill them all or else he is not the Messiah. So the question that either vindicates Jesus or makes him culpable for the world's greatest hoax is, did he fit and fulfill these Old Testament prophecies?

WHAT ARE the ODDS ?

Let's look at two of the specific prophecies about the Messiah in the Old Testament.

> You, O Bethlehem Ephrathah, are only a small village in Judah. Yet a ruler of Israel will come from you, one whose origins are from the distant past. (Micah 5:2, NLT)

> The Lord himself will choose [a] sign. Look! The virgin will conceive a child! She will give birth to a son and will call him Immanuel—"God is with us." (Isaiah 7:14, NLT)

Now, before considering the other 59 prophecies, you have to stop and ask yourself how many people in the category of potential Messiah throughout history were born of a virgin in the town of Bethlehem. "Well, let's see, there's my neighbor George, but … no, never mind; he was born in Brooklyn." In the case of 61 detailed prophecies being fulfilled by one person, we are talking about virtually impossible odds.

When forensic scientists discover a DNA profile match, the odds of having the wrong person is frequently less than one in several billion (something for deviants to keep in mind). It would seem we are in the same neighborhood of odds, and numbers of zeros, in considering a single individual fulfilling these prophecies.

Professor of mathematics Peter Stoner gave 600 students a math probability problem that would determine the odds for one person fulfilling eight specific prophecies. (This is not the same as flipping a coin eight times in a row and getting heads each time.) First the students calculated the odds of one person fulfilling all the conditions of one specific prophecy, such as being betrayed by a friend for 30 pieces of silver. Then the students did their best to estimate the odds for all of the eight prophecies combined.

The students calculated that the odds against one person fulfilling all eight prophecies are astronomical—one in 10^{21}. To illustrate that number, Stoner gave the following example: "First, blanket the entire Earth land mass with silver dollars 120 feet high. Second, specially mark one of those dollars and randomly bury it. Third, ask a person to travel the Earth and select the marked dollar, while blindfolded, from the trillions of other dollars."[7]

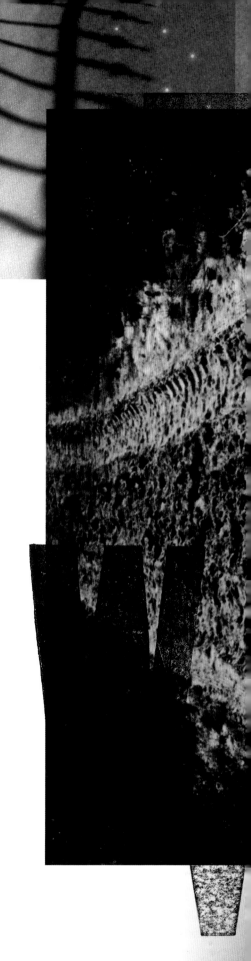

People can do some pretty squishy things with numbers (especially with a last name like that), so it's important to note that Stoner's work was reviewed by the American Scientific Association, which stated, "The mathematical analysis ... is based upon principles of probability which are thoroughly sound, and Professor Stoner has applied these principles in a proper and convincing way." [8]

With that as an introduction, let's add six more predictions to the two we've already considered, giving us a total of Professor Stoner's eight:

Prophecy: The Messiah would be from the lineage of King David.	Jeremiah 23:5	600 B.C.
Fulfillment: "Jesus ... the son of David ..."	Luke 3:23, 31	4 B.C.
Prophecy: The Messiah would be betrayed for 30 pieces of silver.	Zechariah 11:13	487 B.C.
Fulfillment: "They gave him thirty pieces of silver."	Matthew 26:15	30 A.D.
Prophecy: The Messiah would have his hands and feet pierced.	Psalm 22:16	1000 B.C.
Fulfillment: "They came to a place called The Skull. All three were crucified there—Jesus on the center cross, and the two criminals on either side."	Luke 23:33	30 A.D.
Prophecy: People would cast lots for the Messiah's clothing.	Psalm 22:18	1000 B.C.
Fulfillment: "The soldiers ... took his robe, but it was seamless, woven in one piece from the top. So they said, 'Let's not tear it but throw dice to see who gets it.'"	John 19:23-24	30 A.D.
Prophecy: The Messiah would appear riding on a donkey.	Zechariah 9:9	500 B.C.
Fulfillment: "They brought the animals to him and threw their garments over the colt, and he sat on it."	Matthew 21:7	30 A,D.
Prophecy: A messenger would be sent to herald the Messiah.	Malachi 3:1	500 B.C.
Fulfillment: John told them, "I baptize with water, but right here in the crowd is someone you do not know."	John 1:26	27 A.D.

The eight prophecies we've reviewed about the Messiah were written by men from different times and places between about 500 and 1,000 years before Jesus was born. Thus there was no opportunity for collusion among them. Notice too, the specificity. This is not the genre of a Nostradamus prediction—"When the moon turns green, the lima bean will lie cloaked by the roadside."

out of HIS CONTROL

Imagine winning a Powerball lottery with merely one ticket among tens of millions sold. Now imagine winning a hundred of these lotteries in a row. What would people think? Right, "It was rigged!"

And over the years a similar claim has been made by skeptics about Jesus' fulfillment of Old Testament prophecy. They have granted that Jesus fulfilled messianic prophecies but

have accused him of living his life in such a way as to *intentionally* fulfill them. A reasonable objection, but not as plausible as it might seem.

Consider the nature of just four of the messianic prophecies:

- His lineage would come from David (Jeremiah 23:5).
- His birth would occur in Bethlehem (Micah 5:2).
- He would migrate to Egypt (Hosea 11:1).
- He would live in Nazareth (Isaiah 11:1).[9]

Now, what could Jesus do about fulfilling these prophecies? Neither he nor his parents had any control over his ancestry. His birth in Bethlehem was the result of a census mandated by Caesar Augustus. His parents' move to Egypt was prompted by King Herod's persecution. And once Herod died, Jesus' parents naturally decided to resettle in Nazareth.

Even if at a young age an imposter Jesus looked at the prophecies he had accidentally fulfilled and decided to go for it and see if he could make the rest (like someone deciding to shoot the moon in the card game Hearts), the deck would still have been impossibly stacked against him. Consider some of the factors in the prophecies we've already looked at: the Messiah would be betrayed for 30 pieces of silver; he would be killed by means of crucifixion; and people would cast lots for his clothes. These prophecies all came true for Jesus, yet what control did he have over the fulfillment of any of them?

Bible scholars tell us that nearly 300 references to 61 specific prophecies of the Messiah were fulfilled by Jesus Christ. The odds against one person fulfilling that many prophecies would be beyond all mathematical possibility. It could never happen, no matter how much time was allotted. One mathematician's estimate of those impossible odds is "one chance in a trillion, trillion, trillion, trillion, trillion, trillion, trillion, trillion, trillion, trillion, trillion, trillion, trillion."[10]

Bertrand Russell, adamant atheist, was asked in a *Look* magazine interview what evidence it would take for him to believe in God. Russell responded, "Well, if I heard a voice from heaven and it predicted a series of things and they came to pass, then I guess I'd have to believe there's some kind of supernatural being."

Bible scholar Norman Geisler responded to Russell's skepticism. "I'd say, 'Mr. Russell, there has been a voice from heaven; it has

what THE CAVES HELD

In 1947 an Arab boy named Muhammad discovered a limestone cave near the Dead Sea that contained some clay jars. After Muhammad's initial surprise, he discovered that inside the jars were ancient scrolls. No one knew at the time how valuable these scrolls were. Inside those clay jars were well-preserved manuscripts from every Old Testament book except Esther. Most importantly, these were by far the oldest biblical manuscripts scholars had ever seen.

How did these manuscripts get there? Well, it seems they originally belonged to an ascetic religious group called the Essenes (a little like monks of the Middle Ages) who lived in a community near the caves.

The theory goes that the community (called the Qumran community, after their location) came to an end in the late 60s A.D. when Roman troops marched through the area in the process of putting down a Jewish revolt. Quite possibly, all the Essenes were slaughtered at that time. But before that, some of them hid their biblical scrolls and other community documents in caves to preserve them. And there they remained for centuries until a curious boy found them, remarkably unchanged in the dry desert climate.

Archaeologists and paleographers were commissioned to date the documents scientifically. Although these documents were well-preserved copies of the original prophecies written hundreds of year earlier, dating tests confirmed that these copies were transcribed prior to the birth of Jesus. But this meant that the messianic prophecies were written well before Jesus' birth. So paleographers rechecked the dates to make certain. Carbon-dating of the ancient manuscripts proved that the prophetic passages foretelling the Messiah, including the complete writings of Isaiah, preceded the birth of Christ by over a hundred years.

predicted many things; and we've seen them undeniably come to pass.'"[11] Geisler was alluding to the fact that only a transcendent Being outside of time would be able to accurately predict future events.

PROOF IN A JAR

We've looked at the evidence for Jesus' fulfillment of messianic prophecies from every angle but one. What if the Christian scribes who copied scrolls of Isaiah and the other Old Testament prophetic books altered them to make them correspond to Jesus' life?

This is a question many scholars and skeptics have asked. And it seems possible, even plausible at first glance. It would prevent us from making Jesus into a lying imposter, which seems highly unlikely, and it would explain the amazing accuracy of his fulfillment of prophecies. So, how do we know that the Old Testament prophetic books, such as Isaiah, Daniel, and Micah, were written hundreds of years before Christ, as purported? And if they were, how do we know Christians didn't alter the texts later?

For 1,900 years, many skeptics held fast to that theory, based upon the human impossibility of accurately predicting future events. But then something occurred that doused all enthusiasm for such a clandestine conspiracy. Something called the Dead Sea Scrolls.

Half a century back, the finding of the Dead Sea scrolls provided Bible scholars with copies of Old Testament books that were far older than any others known to exist. Extensive tests proved that many of these copies were made *before* Jesus Christ even lived. And they are virtually identical to the texts of the Bible we were already using.

As a result, even scholars who deny Jesus as the Messiah accept these manuscripts of the Old Testament as having predated his birth and therefore concede that the prophecies about the Messiah contained within them have not been altered in order to conform to Jesus.

an INTERESTING TWIST

If these predictions were fulfilled so accurately through the life of Jesus, it seems logical to wonder why everyone in Israel would not have been able to see it. But as his crucifixion attests, not everyone did see it. As the apostle John said of Jesus, "Even in his own land and among his own people, he was not accepted" (John 1:11, NLT).

Of course, many Jews of Jesus' day did recognize him as the Messiah—the entire foundation of the Christian church being Jewish. The majority, however, did not. And it's not so hard to comprehend why. To better understand the first-century Jews' misunderstanding, consider this messianic prophecy written 700 years before the birth of Jesus by the prophet Isaiah. Was it referring to Jesus?

Nearly 300 references to 61 prophecies of the Messiah were fulfilled by Jesus Christ. The odds against one person fulfilling that many prophecies would be beyond all mathematical possibility

THE WORDS OF ISAIAH THE PROPHET: 700 B. C.

All of us have strayed away like sheep. We have left God's paths to follow our own. Yet the Lord laid on him the guilt and sins of us all.

He was oppressed and treated harshly, yet he never said a word. He was led as a lamb to the slaughter. And as a sheep is silent before the shearers, he did not open his mouth. From prison and trial they led him away to his death. But who among the people realized that he was dying for their sins—that he was suffering their punishment? He had done no wrong, and he never deceived anyone. But he was buried like a criminal; he was put in a rich man's grave.

But it was the Lord's good plan to crush him and fill him with grief. Yet when his life is made an offering for sin, he will have a multitude of children, many heirs....And because of what he has experienced, my righteous servant will make it possible for many to be counted righteous, for he will bear all their sins.

(Portions of Isaiah 53:6-11, NLT)

As Jesus hung on the cross, some understandably may have been thinking, How could this be the Messiah? At the same time, others may have been wondering, *Who else but Jesus could Isaiah be talking about?*

IMPOSSIBLE   IMPOSTER

So, what are we to make of Jesus having fulfilled so many prophecies written hundreds of years prior to his birth? Leonardo DiCaprio ... I mean, Frank Abagnale might be a good imposter, but even he got caught by the time he was old enough to drink a beer legally.

Jesus doesn't look anything like a more competent Frank Abagnale. He's in a different category altogether. No imposter could ever beat such odds as those presented by Hebrew prophecy.

And what does that mean? Two conclusions emerge: First, only a transcendent Being could orchestrate such events. And second, it makes all of Jesus' other claims credible and worthy of serious consideration.

In the Gospel of John, Jesus made the claim, "I am the way, the truth and the life." Overwhelming evidence seems to indicate that the signature on that check is not a forgery.

ENDNOTES

[1] Terence Hines, *Pseudoscience and the Paranormal* (Buffalo, NY: Prometheus Books, 2003), 193.

[2] Josh McDowell, *The New Evidence That Demands a Verdict* (San Bernardino, CA: Here's Life Publishers, 1999), 194.

[3] Prediction 3, Quatrain 2, 28.

[4] McDowell, Ibid.

[5] Quoted in McDowell, 12-13.

[6] McDowell, 164-193.

[7] Peter W. Stoner, *Science Speaks* (Chicago: Moody Press, 1958), 97-110.

[8] Stoner, 5.

[9] The Hebrew word *netzer*, appearing in Isaiah 11:1, is believed by many to refer to Nazareth, Jesus' hometown.

[10] Lee Strobel, *The Case for Faith* (Grand Rapids, MI: Zondervan, 2000), 262.

[11] Quoted in Strobel, 141.

BOOK REVIEWS

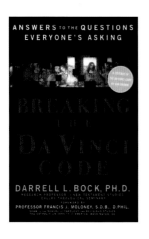

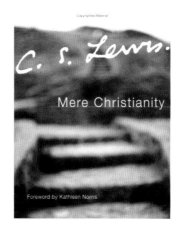

BREAKING THE DA VINCI CODE:
ANSWERS TO THE QUESTIONS EVERYBODY'S ASKING

DARRELL L. BOCK
THOMAS NELSON, 2004,
208 PAGES

New Testament scholar Darrell Bock exposes the shaky foundations of Dan Brown's *The Da Vinci Code*, revealing its nonhistorical elements. Bock goes further by articulating the case for the New Testament's reliability.

As research professor of New Testament studies at Dallas Theological Seminary, Bock is well qualified to speak on the historicity of the New Testament documents, and in this book he reconstructs their development for the layperson. Bock also addresses the mysterious Gnostic Gospels (the basis for much of *The Da Vinci Code*'s conspiracy theory), shedding light on both their content and their reliability.

Anyone who has read *The Da Vinci Code* and wants to measure its theories against the test of history will be well rewarded by reading Bock's analysis.

MERE CHRISTIANITY

C. S. LEWIS
ZONDERVAN, 2001, 240
PAGES

Mere Christianity is a classic in Christian apologetics, having been read and enjoyed by millions of readers since its original publication in the 1940s. Its author, Oxford-educated C. S. Lewis, is regarded as one of the greatest thinkers of the 20th century. Of his many writings, Lewis's *Mere Christianity* has been the most widely read and the most effective in enlightening intellectuals about the rational basis for the Christian faith.

Lewis begins his book by retracing his own steps as a skeptic in his search for truth. Curiously, Lewis did not *begin* his quest for truth with Jesus Christ but rather *concluded* that life could have no ultimate meaning without him. Using humor, imagination, and logic, Lewis conveys thoughts about God and the human condition with insightful illustrations.

This is a must-read for anyone wanting to determine both who Jesus Christ claimed to be and what might be the options for his identity.

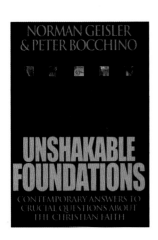

UNSHAKABLE FOUNDATIONS:

CONTEMPORARY ANSWERS TO CRUCIAL QUESTIONS ABOUT THE CHRISTIAN FAITH

NORMAN GEISLER &
PETER BOCCHINO
BETHANY HOUSE, 2001,
413 PAGES

For the more serious student, this book not only shows how Christianity survives every postmodern attack but also provides compelling reasons for why Christianity is the only solution for the human dilemma.

Geisler and Bocchino show how the Christian worldview transcends logic, science, macroevolution, law, justice, evil, history, ethics, and 21st-century social issues.

To make the difficult subject matter more relevant and comprehensible, the authors have provided numerous illustrations and analogies. A foundational book in Christian apologetics.

THE CASE FOR CHRIST:

A JOURNALIST'S PERSONAL INVESTIGATION OF THE EVIDENCE FOR JESUS

LEE STROBEL
ZONDERVAN, 1998, 304
PAGES

Lee Strobel, a former atheist with a degree from Yale Law School, launches his personal investigation into the evidence for Jesus Christ and the case for Christianity. As a trained legal journalist, Strobel evaluates both sides of the Jesus debate to arrive at a rational verdict about Jesus, based upon the evidence.

Throughout the book, Strobel records actual interviews with scholars as he asks them tough, penetrating questions about the case for Christ.

This book is a starting point for anyone wanting to conduct a personal investigation into Jesus and his claims. Informative and compelling.

BODY COUNT

EXPLAINING THE DISAPPEARANCE AND REAPPEARANCE OF JESUS?

Atheist Bertrand Russell, who doubted Jesus' very existence, assumed that the resurrection of the body was impossible. In 1926, Russell wrote, "I believe that when I die I shall rot, and nothing of my own ego will survive."[1] Well, that's cheerful. Russell clearly bordered on the morose, but we've all wondered, with perhaps more optimism, what will happen to us when we die.

> "BUDDHA IS DEAD. MOHAMMAD IS DEAD. MOSES IS DEAD. CONFUCIUS IS DEAD. BUT ACCORDING TO CHRISTIANITY... CHRIST IS ALIVE."
>
> R. C. SPROUL

Death has been called "the great equalizer." Thousands of stone markers surrounded by spacious green lawns tell the stories. Nobel Prize winners. Beauty queens. Billionaires. Presidents. All die. Someday it will be our turn. Are we to despair with Russell, or is there hope? According to the New Testament, Jesus' resurrection has given us hope for eternal life beyond the grave. All of Christianity hinges on that one promise.

Theologian R. C. Sproul has stated, "The claim of resurrection is vital to Christianity. If Christ has been raised from the dead by God, then He has the credentials and certification that no other religious leader possesses. Buddha is dead. Mohammad is dead. Moses is dead. Confucius is dead. But, according to … Christianity, Christ is alive."[2]

So different and so abnormal is all this that a part of us would like to dismiss it as myth. But is the resurrection to be relegated to a Sunday school story—or is there evidence?

Researcher Josh McDowell said, "After more than seven hundred hours of studying this subject and thoroughly investigating its foundation, I have come to the conclusion that the resurrection of Jesus Christ is one of the most wicked, vicious, heartless hoaxes ever foisted upon the minds of men, OR it is the most fantastic fact of history."[3] Right. So which is it?

Let's look at the evidence.

CYNICS AND SKEPTICS

But not everyone is willing to fairly examine the evidence. Bertrand Russell admits his take on Jesus was "not concerned" with historical facts.[4] Historian Joseph Campbell, without citing evidence, calmly told his PBS television audience that the resurrection of Jesus is not a factual event.[5] Other scholars, such as John Dominic Crossan of the Jesus Seminar, agree with him.[6] None of these skeptics present any evidence for their views.

To be honest, the thought that anyone could be dead for three days, and then come back to life is cause for a strong dose of skepticism. But whereas cynics are closed minded to the facts, according to *Skeptic* magazine, true skeptics always keep their minds open to the evidence. An editorial in the magazine states, "When we say we are 'skeptical,' we mean that we must see compelling evidence before we believe."[7]

As our cold case of Jesus' resurrection gets underway, let's put ourselves in the role of a skeptic who needs compelling evidence before we will believe such an incredible event really occurred.

SELF-PROPHECY

In advance of his death, Jesus told his disciples that he would be betrayed, arrested, and crucified and that he would come back to life three days later. That's a strange plan! What was behind it? Jesus was no entertainer willing to perform for others on demand; instead, he promised that his death and resurrection would prove to people (if their minds and hearts were open) that he was indeed the Messiah.

Bible scholar Wilbur Smith remarked about Jesus,

When he said that He himself would rise again from the dead, the third day after He was crucified, He said something that only a fool would dare say, if He expected longer the devotion of any disciples—unless He was sure He was going to rise. No founder of any world religion known to men ever dared say a thing like that.[8]

In other words, since Jesus had clearly told his disciples that he would rise again after his death, failure to keep that promise would expose him as a fraud. So let's begin our skeptical inquiry of the resurrection with the events surrounding Jesus' death and burial.

WHAT SHOULD HAVE BEEN THE END OF THE STORY

You know what Jesus' last hours of earthly life were like if you watched the movie by road warrior/braveheart Mel Gibson. If you missed parts of *The Passion of the Christ* because you were shielding your eyes (it would have been easier to simply shoot the movie with a red filter on the camera), just flip to the back pages of any Gospel in your New Testament to find out what you missed.

As Jesus predicted, he was betrayed by one of his own disciples, Judas Iscariot, and was arrested. In a mock trial under the Roman governor Pontius Pilate, he was convicted of treason and condemned to die on a wooden cross. Prior to being nailed to the cross, Jesus was brutally beaten with a Roman cat-o'-nine-tails, a whip with bits of bone and metal that would rip flesh. He was punched repeatedly, kicked, and spit upon.

Then, using mallets, the Roman executioners pounded the heavy wrought-iron nails into Jesus' wrists and feet. Finally they dropped the cross in a hole in the ground between two other crosses bearing convicted thieves.

Jesus hung there for approximately six hours. Then, at 3:00 in the afternoon—that is, at exactly the same time the Passover lamb was being sacrificed as a sin offering—Jesus cried out, "It is finished" (in Aramaic), and died. Suddenly the sky went dark and an earthquake shook the land.[9]

Pilate wanted verification that Jesus was dead before allowing his crucified body to be buried. So a Roman guard thrust a spear into Jesus' side. The mixture of blood and water that flowed out was a clear indication that Jesus was dead. Jesus' body was then taken down from the cross and buried in Joseph of Arimathea's tomb. Roman

"THE SILENCE OF HISTORY IS DEAFENING WHEN IT COMES TO THE TESTIMONY AGAINST THE RESURRECTION."

TOM ANDERSON
FORMER PRESIDENT,
CALIFORNIA TRIAL LAWYERS
ASSOCIATION

guards next sealed the tomb and secured it with a 24-hour watch.

Meanwhile, Jesus' disciples were in shock. Dr. J. P. Moreland writes of their mental state. "They no longer had confidence that Jesus had been sent by God. They also had been taught that God would not let his Messiah suffer death. So they dispersed. The Jesus movement was all but stopped in its tracks."[10]

SOMETHING HAPPENED

But it wasn't the end. The Jesus movement did not disappear (obviously), and in fact Christianity exists today as the world's largest religion. Therefore, we've got to know what happened after Jesus' body was taken down from the cross and laid in the tomb.

In a *New York Times* article, Peter Steinfels cites the startling events that occurred three days after Jesus' death: "Shortly after Jesus was executed, his followers were suddenly galvanized from a baffled and cowering group into people whose message about a living Jesus and a coming kingdom, preached at the risk of their lives, eventually changed an empire. Something happened… But exactly what?"[11] That's the question we have to answer with an investigation into the facts.

There are only five plausible explanations for Jesus' alleged resurrection, as portrayed in the New Testament:

1. Jesus didn't really die on the cross.
2. The "resurrection" was a conspiracy.
3. The disciples were hallucinating.
4. The account is legendary.
5. It really happened.

Let's work our way through these options and see which one best fits the facts.

WAS JESUS DEAD?

"Marley was deader than a doornail, of that there was no doubt." So begins Charles Dickens's *A Christmas Carol*, the author not wanting anyone to be mistaken as to the supernatural character of what is soon to take place. In the same way, before we take on the role of CSI and piece together evidence for a resurrection, we must first establish that there was, in fact, a corpse. After all, occasionally the newspapers will report on some "corpse" in a morgue who was found stirring and recovered. Could something like that have happened with Jesus?

Some have proposed that Jesus lived through the crucifixion and was revived by the cool, damp air in the tomb–"Whoa, how long was I out for?" But that theory doesn't seem to square with the medical evidence. An article in the *Journal of the American Medical Association* explains why this so-called "swoon theory" is untenable: "Clearly, the weight of historical and medical evidence indicated that Jesus was dead. … The spear, thrust between His right ribs, probably perforated not only the right lung but also the pericardium and heart and thereby ensured His death."[12] But skepticism of this verdict may be in order, as this case has been cold for 2,000 years. At the very least, we need a second opinion.

One place to find that is in the reports of non-Christian historians from around the time when Jesus lived. Three of these historians mentioned the death of Jesus.

- Lucian (c.120–after 180 A.D.) referred to Jesus as a crucified sophist (philosopher).[13]
- Josephus (c.37–c.100A.D.) wrote, "At this time there appeared Jesus, a wise man, for he was a doer of amazing deeds. When Pilate condemned him to the cross, the leading men among us, having accused him, those who loved him did not cease to do so."[14]
- Tacitus (c. 56–c.120 A.D.) wrote, "Christus, from whom the name had its origin, suffered the extreme penalty … at the hands of our procurator Pontius Pilate."[15]

"AFTER JESUS WAS EXECUTED, HIS FOLLOWERS WERE SUDDENLY GALVANIZED FROM A BAFFLED AND COWERING GROUP INTO PEOPLE WHOSE MESSAGE ABOUT A LIVING JESUS.... EVENTUALLY CHANGED AN EMPIRE. SOMETHING HAPPENED.... BUT EXACTLY WHAT?"
–PETER STEINFELS, NEW YORK TIMES

This is a bit like going into the archives and finding that on one spring day in the first century *The Jerusalem Post* ran a front-page story saying that Jesus was crucified and dead. Not bad detective work, and fairly conclusive.

In fact, there is no historical account from Christians, Romans, or Jews that disputes either Jesus' death or his burial. Even Crossan, a skeptic of the resurrection, agrees that Jesus really lived and died: "That he was crucified is as sure as anything historical can ever be."[16] In light of such evidence, we seem to be on good grounds for dismissing the first of our five options. Jesus was clearly dead, "of that there was no doubt."

THE MATTER OF AN EMPTY TOMB

No serious historian really doubts Jesus was dead when he was taken down from the cross. However, many have questioned how Jesus' body disappeared from the tomb. English journalist Dr. Frank Morison initially thought the resurrection was either

FRANK MORISON AND THE EXPOSÉ THAT NEVER WAS

In the early 1900s, German criticism of the Bible and the rationalist movement were sweeping over Western Europe and the United States, carrying with them the belief that nothing can happen apart from natural laws. With that naturalistic belief came a skepticism toward the foundation of Christianity—the resurrection of Jesus Christ.

One who was greatly influenced by such skepticism was English journalist Frank Morison, who came to believe that the story of Jesus rising from the dead was nothing more than a fairy tale for adults.

Morison decided to investigate the facts surrounding Jesus' supposed resurrection, fully expecting to discover a story full of holes, missing evidence, and illogical conclusions. He then would write a book exposing the myth. This notable journalist wrote of his intent:

I wanted to take this last phase of the life of Jesus, with all its quick and pulsating drama, its sharp, clear-cut background of antiquity, and its tremendous psychological and human interest—to strip it of its overgrowth of primitive beliefs and dogmatic suppositions, and to see this supremely great Person as He really was.[17]

But Morison was stunned by what he discovered. He ex claimed, "The book as it was originally planned was left high and dry."[18] Morison's book—*Who Moved the Stone?*—did finally get written, but it had an entirely different ending than he had intended.

a myth or a hoax, and he began research to write a book refuting it.[19] The book became famous but for reasons other than its original intent, as we'll see.

Morison began by attempting to solve the case of the empty tomb. The tomb belonged to a member of the Sanhedrin Council, Joseph of Arimathea. In Israel at that time, to be on the council was to be a rock star. Everyone knew who was on the council. Joseph must have been a real person. Otherwise, the Jewish leaders would have exposed the story as a fraud in their attempt to disprove the resurrection. Also, Joseph's tomb would have been at a well-known location and easily identifiable, so any thoughts of Jesus being "lost in the graveyard" would need to be dismissed.

Morison wondered why Jesus' enemies would have allowed the "empty tomb myth" to persist if it wasn't true. The discovery of Jesus' body would have instantly killed the entire plot.

And what is known historically of Jesus' enemies is that they accused Jesus' disciples of stealing the body, an accusation clearly predicated on a shared belief that the tomb was empty.

Dr. Paul L. Maier, professor of ancient history at Western Michigan University, similarly stated, "If all the evidence is weighed carefully and fairly, it is indeed justifiable ... to conclude that the tomb in which Jesus was buried was actually empty on the morning of the first Easter. And no shred of evidence has yet been discovered ... that would disprove this statement."[20]

The Jewish leaders were stunned and accused the disciples of stealing Jesus' body. But the Romans had assigned a 24-hour watch at the tomb with a trained guard unit (from 4 to 12 soldiers). Morison asked, "How could these professionals have let Jesus' body be vandalized?" It would have been impossible for anyone to have slipped by the Roman guards and to have moved a two-ton stone. Yet the stone was moved away and the body of Jesus was missing.

If Jesus' body was anywhere to be found, his enemies would have quickly exposed the resurrection as a fraud. Tom Anderson, former president of the California Trial Lawyers Association, summarizes the strength of this argument:

> With an event so well publicized, don't you think that it's reasonable that one historian, one eye witness, one antagonist would record for all time that he had seen Christ's body? ... The silence of history is deafening when it comes to the testimony against the resurrection.[21]

So, with no body of evidence, and with a known tomb clearly empty, Morison accepted the evidence as solid that Jesus' body had somehow disappeared from the tomb.

GRAVE ROBBING?

As Morison continued his investigation, he began to examine the motives of Jesus' followers. Maybe the supposed resurrection was actually a stolen body. But if so, how does one account for all the reported appearances of a resurrected Jesus? Historian Paul Johnson, in *History of the Jews*, wrote, "What mattered was not the circumstances

of his death but the fact that he was widely and obstinately believed, by an expanding circle of people, to have risen again."[22] The tomb was indeed empty. But it wasn't the mere absence of a body that could have galvanized Jesus' followers (especially if they had been the ones who had stolen it). Something extraordinary must have happened, for the followers of Jesus ceased mourning, ceased hiding, and began fearlessly proclaiming that they had seen Jesus alive.

Each eyewitness account reports that Jesus suddenly appeared bodily to his followers, the women first. Morison wondered why conspirators would make women central to its plot. In the first century, women had virtually no rights, personhood, or status. If the plot was to succeed, Morison reasoned, the conspirators would have portrayed men, not women, as the first to see Jesus alive. And yet we hear that women touched him, spoke with him, and were the first to find the empty tomb.

Later, according to the eyewitness accounts, all the disciples saw Jesus on more than ten separate occasions. They wrote that he showed them his hands and feet and told them to touch him. And he reportedly ate with them and later appeared alive to more than 500 followers on one occasion.

Legal scholar John Warwick Montgomery stated, "In 56 A.D. [the apostle] Paul wrote that over 500 people had seen the risen Jesus and that most of them were still alive (1 Corinthians 15:6ff.). It passes the bounds of credibility that the early Christians could have manufactured such a tale and then preached it among those who might easily have refuted it simply by producing the body of Jesus."[23]

Bible scholars Geisler and Turek agree. "If the Resurrection had not occurred, why would the apostle Paul give such a list of supposed eyewitnesses? He would immediately lose all credibility with his Corinthian readers by lying so blatantly."[24]

British Bible scholar Michael Green remarked, "The appearances of Jesus are as well authenticated as anything in antiquity. ... There can be no rational doubt that they occurred."[25]

CONSISTENT TO THE END

As if the eyewitness reports were not enough to challenge Morison's skepticism, he was also baffled by the disciples' behavior. A fact of history that has stumped historians, psychologists, and skeptics alike is that these 11 former cowards were suddenly willing to suffer humiliation, torture, and death. All but one of Jesus' disciples were slain as martyrs. Would they have done so much for a lie, knowing they had taken the body?

The Islamic martyrs on September 11 proved that some will die for a false cause they believe in. Yet to be a willing martyr for a known lie is insanity. As Paul Little wrote, "Men will die for what they believe to be true, though it may actually be false. They do not, however, die for what they know is a lie."[26] Jesus' disciples behaved in a manner consistent with a genuine belief that their leader was alive.

No one has adequately explained why the disciples would have been willing to die for a known lie. But even if they all conspired to lie about Jesus' resurrection, how could they have kept the conspiracy going for decades without at least one of them selling out for money or position? Moreland wrote, "Those who lie for personal gain do not stick together very long, especially when hardship decreases the benefits."[27]

Chuck Colson, implicated in the Watergate scandal, pointed out the difficulty of several people maintaining a lie for an extended period of time.

> I know the resurrection is a fact, and Watergate proved it to me. How? Because 12 men testified they had seen Jesus raised from the dead, then they proclaimed that truth for 40 years, never once denying it. Every one was beaten, tortured, stoned and put in prison. They would not have endured that if it weren't true. Watergate embroiled 12 of the most powerful men in the world—and they couldn't keep a lie for three weeks. You're telling me 12 apostles could keep a lie for 40 years? Absolutely impossible.[28]

Something happened that changed everything for these men and women. Morison acknowledged, "Whoever comes to this problem has sooner or later to confront a fact that

cannot be explained away. ... This fact is that ... a profound conviction came to the little group of people—a change that attests to the fact that Jesus had risen from the grave."[29]

A BAD TRIP?

Sometimes certain people can "see" things they want to, things that aren't really there. And that's why some have claimed that the disciples were so distraught over the crucifixion that their desire to see Jesus alive caused mass hallucination. Plausible?

Psychologist Gary Collins, former president of the American Association of Christian Counselors, was asked about the possibility that hallucinations were behind the disciples' radically changed behavior. Collins remarked, "Hallucinations are individual occurrences. By their very nature only one person can see a given hallucination at a time. They certainly aren't something which can be seen by a group of people."[30]

Hallucination is not even a remote possibility, according to psychologist Thomas J. Thorburn. "It is absolutely inconceivable that ... five hundred persons, of average soundness of mind ... should experience all kinds of sensuous impressions—visual, auditory, tactual—and that all these ... experiences should rest entirely upon ... hallucination."[31]

LEGEND?

Some unconvinced skeptics attribute the resurrection story to a legend on a par with King Arthur's round table, or Robin Hood.

But there are three major problems with that theory.

1. Legends rarely develop while multiple eyewitnesses are alive to refute them. One historian of ancient Rome and Greece, A. N. Sherwin-White, argued that the resurrection news spread too soon and too quickly for it to have been a legend. [32]

2. Legends develop by oral tradition and don't come with contemporary historical documents that can be verified. Yet the Gospels were written within three decades of the resurrection. [33]

3. The legend theory doesn't adequately explain either the fact of the empty tomb or the historically verified conviction of the apostles that Jesus was alive. [34]

WHY DID CHRISTIANITY WIN?

Morison was bewildered by the fact that "a tiny insignificant movement was able to prevail over the cunning grip of the Jewish establishment, as well as the might of Rome." Why did it win, in the face of all those odds against it?

He wrote, "Within twenty years the claim of these Galilean peasants had disrupted the Jewish church. … In less than fifty years it had begun to threaten the peace of the Roman Empire. When we have said everything that can be said … we stand confronted with the greatest mystery of all. Why did it win?" [35]

By all rights, Christianity should have died out at the cross when the disciples fled for their lives. But the apostles went on to establish a growing Christian movement.

J. N. D. Anderson wrote, "Think of the psychological absurdity of picturing a little band of defeated cowards cowering in an upper room one day and a few days later transformed into a company that no persecution could silence—and then attempting to attribute this dramatic change to nothing more convincing than a miserable fabrication. … That simply wouldn't make sense." [36]

Many scholars believe (in the words of an ancient commentator) that "the blood of the martyrs was the seed of the church." Historian Will Durant observed, "Caesar and Christ had met in the arena and Christ had won." [37]

A SURPRISE CONCLUSION

Morison became convinced that his preconceived bias against Jesus Christ's resurrection had been wrong. He began writing a different book—entitled *Who Moved the Stone?*—to detail his new conclusions. Morison simply followed the trail of evidence, clue by clue, until the truth of the case seemed clear to him. His surprise was that the evidence led to a belief in the resurrection. He writes, "It was as though a man set out to cross a forest by a familiar and well-beaten track and came out suddenly where he did not expect to come out." [38]

Morison is not alone. Countless other skeptics have examined the evidence for Jesus' resurrection, and accepted it as the most astounding fact in all of human history. But the resurrection of Jesus Christ brings us back to the question: What does the fact that Jesus defeated death have to do with my life? The answer to that question is what New Testament Christianity is all about. (See article 7)

"A TINY INSIGNIFICANT MOVEMENT WAS ABLE TO PREVAIL OVER THE CUNNING GRIP OF THE JEWISH ESTABLISHMENT AS WELL AS THE MIGHT OF ROME….WE STAND CONFRONTED WITH THE GREATEST MYSTERY OF ALL. WHY DID IT WIN?" FRANK MORISON, ENGLISH JOURNALIST

COULD THIS BE JESUS' TOMB?

ENDNOTES

1 Paul Edwards, "Great Minds: Bertrand Russell," *Free Inquiry*, December 2004/January 2005, 46.

2 R. C. Sproul, *Reason to Believe* (Grand Rapids, MI: Lamplighter, 1982), 44.

3 Josh McDowell, *The New Evidence That Demands a Verdict* (San Bernardino, CA: Here's Life, 1999), 203.

4 Bertrand Russell, *Why I Am Not a Christian* (New York: Simon & Schuster, 1957), 16.

5 Joseph Campbell, an interview with Bill Moyers, *Joseph Campbell and the Power of Myth*, PBS TV special, 1988.

6 Michael J. Wilkins and J. P. Moreland, eds, *Jesus Under Fire* (Grand Rapids, MI: Zondervan, 1995), 2.

7 "What Is a Skeptic?" editorial in *Skeptic*, vol 11, no. 2), 5.

8 McDowell, *New Evidence*, 209.

9 Historian Will Durant reported, "About the middle of this first century a pagan named Thallus … argued that the abnormal darkness alleged to have accompanied the death of Christ was a purely natural phenomenon and coincidence; the argument took the existence of Christ for granted. The denial of that existence never seems to have occurred even to the bitterest gentile or Jewish opponents of nascent Christianity." Will Durant, *Caesar and Christ*, vol. 3 of The Story of Civilization (New York: Simon & Schuster, 1972), 555.

10 Quoted in Lee Strobel, *The Case for Christ* (Grand Rapids, MI: Zondervan, 1998), 246.

11 Peter Steinfels, "Jesus Died—And Then What Happened?" *New York Times*, April 3, 1988, E9.

12 Quoted in McDowell, *New Evidence*, 224.

13 Quoted in McDowell, *Evidence*, 82.

14 McDowell, 82.

15 McDowell, 81, 82.

16 Gary R. Habermas and Michael R. Licona, *The Case for the Resurrection of Jesus* (Grand Rapids, MI: Kregel, 2004), 49.

17 Frank Morison, *Who Moved the Stone?* (Grand Rapids, MI: Lamplighter, 1958), back cover.

18 Morison, preface, 8.

19 Morison, 9.

20 Quoted in Josh McDowell, *The Resurrection Factor* (San Bernardino, CA: Here's Life, 1981), 10.

21 Quoted in McDowell, *The Resurrection Factor*, 66.

22 Paul Johnson, *A History of the Jews* (New York: Harper & Row, 1988), 130.

23 Quoted in McDowell, *New Evidence*, 249.

24 Norman L. Geisler and Frank Turek, *I Don't Have Enough Faith to Be an Atheist* (Wheaton, IL: Crossway, 2004), 243.

25 Michael Green, *The Empty Cross of Jesus* (Downers Grove, IL: InterVarsity, 1984), 97, quoted in John Ankerberg and John Weldon, *Knowing the Truth about the Resurrection* (Eugene, OR: Harvest House), 22.

26 Paul Little, *Know Why You Believe* (Wheaton, IL: Victor, 1967), 44.

27 J. P. Moreland, *Scaling the Secular City*, (Grand Rapids, MI: Baker Book House, 2000), 172.

28 Charles Colson, "The Paradox of Power," Power to Change, www.powertochange. ie/changed/index_Leaders.

29 Morison, 104.

30 Quoted in Strobel, 238.

31 Quoted in McDowell, *New Evidence*, 274.

32 Quoted in *Jesus Under Fire*, 154.

33 Habermas, 85.

34 Habermas, 87.

35 Morison, 115.

36 Quoted in McDowell, 249.

37 Durant, 652.

38 McDowell, *Resurrection Factor*, 111.

39 Quoted in McDowell, 11.

40 Quoted in McDowell 9.

A STUNNED PROFESSOR

A skeptic of the resurrection, Simon Greenleaf (1783–1853) helped to put the Harvard Law School on the map. He wrote *A Treatise on the Law of Evidence*, which is still regarded as one of the outstanding works on establishing legal evidence. Professor Greenleaf had stated to his Harvard law class that the resurrection of Jesus Christ is a legend. In a rebuttal, three of his law students challenged him to apply his acclaimed rules of evidence to the resurrection account.

Greenleaf accepted the students' challenge. Yet this expert in evaluating evidence was unable to explain the dramatic change in the behavior of the disciples without assuming the truth of the resurrection. Greenleaf reasoned that no group of people could have maintained their story through such persecution unless they knew it was true.[39]

After systematically evaluating the evidence, the Harvard law professor reversed his bias against the resurrection, concluding, "There is more evidence for the historical fact of the resurrection of Jesus Christ than for just about any other event in history."[40]

WHY JESUS?
IS HE RELEVANT TODAY?

In the February, 2006 cover story, "The Passion of Kanye West," *Rolling Stone* magazine features Grammy award winner West with a crown of thorns on his head. The image is a parody of Jim Caviezel's portrayal of Jesus in *The Passion of the Christ*.

Although West is known for his irreverence, having drawn fire for suggesting that he should be "a part of the Bible," a near fatal automobile accident in 2002 set him on a search for life's meaning. In his hit, "Jesus Walks," West reveals an inner struggle where he admits that the wrongs in his life have kept God distant, yet he still speaks of his need for Jesus. A few verses in the rap tune, "Jesus Walks," relate West's struggle:[1]

I ain't here to argue about his facial features
Or here to convert atheists into believers
I'm just tryin to say the way school need teachers
The way Kathy Lee needed Regis that's the way yall need Jesus...

And I don't think there's nothing I can do to right my wrongs
Jesus Walks with me with me with me with me
I wanna talk to God but I'm afraid cause we ain't spoke in so long ...

To Kanye West, Jesus is real, but irrelevant to his personal guilt and need to connect with God. If Jesus is who he claimed to be, the Creator of life, we would expect him to be relevant to our lives. In fact, Jesus said that he came to bring us a life beyond our wildest dreams. If that is true, we would expect him to provide answers to our innermost questions:

- "Who am I?"
- "Why am I here?"
- "Where am I going?"

"Who am I" is a question that shockingly confronted Academy Award winner Jack Nicholson. Abandoned by his father as an infant, Nicholson was led to believe that his grandmother was his mother and his mother was his older sister. He grew up believing their story until at the age of 37 a *Time* magazine researcher exposed the truth.

Left without a sense of his own roots, Nicholson sought his identity in pleasure---living for the moment. He states, "I resist all established beliefs. My religion basically is to be immediate, to live in the now... I envy people of faith....I pray to something...up there....It's part of being human, I guess."[2]

Madonna attempted to answer the question of, "Why am I here?" by becoming a diva, confessing, "There were many years when I thought fame, fortune, and public approval would bring me happiness. But one day you wake up and realize they don't....I still felt something was missing....I wanted to know the meaning of true and lasting happiness and how I could go about finding it."[3]

"There were many years when I thought fame, fortune, and public approval would bring me happiness. But one day you wake up and realize they don't.... I still felt something was missing..."

MADONNA

Others have given up on finding meaning. Kurt Cobain, lead singer of the Seattle grunge band Nirvana, despaired of life at age 27 and committed suicide. Jazz-age cartoonist Ralph Barton also found life to be meaningless, leaving the following suicide note: "I have had few difficulties, many friends, great successes; I have gone from wife to wife, and from house to house, visited countries of the world, but I am fed up with inventing devices to fill up 24 hours of the day."[4]

Pascal, the great French philosopher believed this inner void we all experience can only be filled by God. He states, "There is a God-shaped vacuum in the heart of every man which only Jesus Christ can fill."[5] If Pascal is right, then we would expect Jesus to not only answer the question of our identity and meaning in this life, but also to give us hope for life after we die.

Can there be meaning, without God? Not according to atheist Bertrand Russell, who wrote, "Unless you assume a god, the question of life's purpose is meaningless."[6] Russell resigned himself to ultimately "rot" in the grave. In his book, *Why I am not a Christian,* Russell dismissed everything Jesus said about life's meaning, including his promise of eternal life.

But if Jesus actually defeated death as eyewitnesses claim, (see article 6) then he alone would be able to tell us what life is all about, and answer, "Where am I going?" In order to understand how Jesus' words, life, and death can establish our identities, give us meaning in life, and provide hope for the future, we need to understand what he said about God, about us, and about himself.

WHAT DID JESUS SAY ABOUT GOD?

Relational

Jesus told us and showed us what God is like. Many think of God more as a force than a person who we can know and enjoy. The God of whom Jesus spoke is not like the impersonal Force in *Star Wars*, whose goodness is measured in voltage. On the contrary, He is relational like us, but even more so. He thinks, He hears. He communicates in language we can understand. And Jesus told us that God is loving.

Loving

God's love is radically different from ours in that it is not based upon attraction or performance. It is totally sacrificial and unselfish. Jesus compared God's love with the love of a perfect father. A good father wants the best for his children, sacrifices for them, and provides for them. But in their best interests, he also disciplines them.

Jesus illustrates God's heart of love with a story about a rebellious son who rejected his father's advice about life and what is important. Arrogant and self-willed, the son wanted to quit working and "live it up." Rather than waiting until his father was ready to give him his inheritance, he began insisting that his father give it to him early.

In Jesus' story, the father granted his son's request. But things went bad for the son. After squandering his money on self-indulgence, the rebellious son had to go to work on a pig farm. Soon he was so hungry even the pig food looked good. Despondent and not sure his father would accept him back, he packed his bag and headed home.

Jesus tells us that not only did his father welcome him home, but he actually ran out to meet him. And then the father went totally radical with his love and threw a huge party celebrating his son's return.

It is interesting that even though the father greatly loved his son, he didn't chase after him. He let the son he loved feel pain and suffer the consequences of his rebellious choice. In a similar way, the Scriptures teach that God's love will never compromise what is best for us. It will allow us to suffer the consequences of our own wrong choices.

Jesus also taught that God will never compromise His character. Character is who we are down deep. It is our essence from which all our thoughts and actions stem. So what is God like—down deep?

Holy

Throughout the Scriptures (nearly 600 times), God is spoken of as "holy." Holy means that God's character is morally pure and perfect in every way. Unblemished. This means that He never entertains a thought that is impure or inconsistent with His moral excellence.

Furthermore, God's holiness means that He cannot be in the presence of evil. Since evil is the opposite of His nature, He hates it. It's like pollution to Him.

The Passion Of The Christ

Watching Jim Caviezel portray Jesus in Mel Gibson's The Passion of the Christ is a gut-wrenching experience. Sadistic Roman guards take turns brutally beating the blindfolded Jesus, taunting him to identify which person did it. Then, after delivering a horrific beating with barbed whips, his executioners nail his hands and feet to a wooden cross. Hours later, Jesus dies, following hours of indescribable suffering. It's enough to make even the most calloused viewers wince. Many stunned viewers were left wondering what it was all about.

The movie never really answers that question, but fortunately the New Testament does. Paul told the Roman Christians that, "God showed his great love for us by sending Christ to die for us while we were still sinners." Since that event nearly two thousand years ago, billions have accepted Jesus' gift and committed their lives to him. And from the first Christians on into the 21st century, Jesus has changed lives. One of those lives that changed dramatically came as a result of watching The Passion of the Christ.

On January 19, 2004, the Fort Bend County sheriff's office received a tragic call: Renee Coulter had discovered her 19-year-old daughter, Ashley Wilson, dead in her apartment. A pillowcase was over her head, and a cord was wrapped around her neck. All the evidence seemed to point to suicide.

In March 2004, less than six weeks after Ashley's death, The Passion of the Christ came to Richmond, Texas. Dan Leach purchased a ticket and went into the theater for an experience that would change his life forever. Almost immediately after watching the movie, twenty-one-year-old Leach, walked into the Fort Bend County sheriff's office and turned himself in for the murder of Ashley Wilson.

The police were stunned, thinking her death was a suicide. But Dan Leach convinced them otherwise. In an exclusive interview with KTRH radio in Houston, Leach revealed that in seeing and understanding Christ's death, he was led to confess. In a remarkable turn of events, Jesus had changed another life.

I'd be in big trouble if Karma was going to finally be my judge....
Bono, U2

But if God is holy and abhors evil, why didn't He make our character like His? Why are there child molesters, murderers, rapists, and perverts? And why do we struggle so with our own moral choices? That brings us to the next part of our quest for meaning. What did Jesus say about *us*?

WHAT DID JESUS SAY ABOUT US?

Made for a Relationship with Him

If you were to read through the New Testament you would discover that Jesus continually spoke of our immense value to God, telling us that God created us to be His children.

Irish U2 rock star Bono remarked in an interview, "It's a mind-blowing concept that the God who created the Universe might be looking for company, a real relationship with people...."[7] In other words, before the universe was created, God planned to adopt us into His family. Not only that, but He has planned an incredible inheritance that is ours for the taking. Like the father's heart in Jesus' story, God wants to lavish on us an inheritance of unimaginable blessing and royal privilege. In His eyes, we are special.

Freedom to Choose

In the movie, *Stepford Wives*, weak, lying, greedy and murderous men have engineered submissive, obedient robots to replace their liberated wives who they considered threats. Although the men supposedly love their wives, they replaced them with *toys* in order to force their obedience.

God could have made us like that — robotic people (iPeople) hardwired to love and obey him, programming worship into us like a screensaver. But then our compulsory love would be meaningless. He wanted us to love Him freely. In real relationships, we want someone to love us for who we are, not out of compulsion — we'd prefer a soul mate over a mail-order bride. Søren Kierkegaard summarized the dilemma in this story.

> Suppose there was a king who loved a humble maiden. The king was like no other king. Every statesman trembled before his power ... and yet this mighty king was melted by love for a humble maiden. How could he declare his love for her? In an odd sort of way, his kingliness tied his hands. If he brought her to the palace and crowned her head with jewels ... she would surely not resist—no one dared resist him. But would she love him? She would say she loved him of course, but would she truly?[8]

You see the problem. Less poetically put: How do you break up with an all-knowing boyfriend? ("It's just not working out between us, but I guess you already knew that.") But to make freely exchanged love possible, God created human beings with a unique capacity: free will.

Rebels

C.S. Lewis reasoned that even though we are internally programmed with a desire to know God, we rebel against it from the moment we are born.[9] Lewis also began to examine his own motives, which led him to the discovery that he instinctively knew right from wrong. This recognition that we are programmed with an inner moral law led the former atheist to the conclusion there must be a moral "Lawgiver."

Indeed, according to both Jesus and the Scriptures, God has given us a moral law to obey. And not only have we turned our backs on a relationship with Him, we also have broken these moral laws that God established. Most of us know some of the Ten Commandments: "Don't lie, steal, murder, commit adultery," etc. Jesus summarized them by saying we should love God with all our heart and our neighbor as ourselves. Sin, therefore, is not only the wrong that we do in breaking the law, but also our failure to do what is right.

God made the universe with laws that govern everything in it. They are inviolable and unchangeable. When Einstein derived the formula $E=MC^2$ he unlocked the mystery of nuclear energy. Put the right ingredients together under exacting conditions and enormous power is unleashed. The Scriptures tell us that God's moral law is no less valid since it stems from His very character.

From the very first man and woman, we have disobeyed God's laws, even though they are for our best. And we have failed to do what is right. We have inherited this condition from the first man, Adam. The

Bible calls this disobedience, *sin*, which means "missing the mark," like an archer missing his intended target. Thus our sins have broken His intended relationship with us. Using the archer's example, we have missed the mark when it comes to the purpose we were created for.

Sin causes the severing of all relationships: the human race severed from its environment (alienation), individuals severed from themselves (guilt and shame), people severed from other people (war, murder), and people severed from God (spiritual death). Like links on a chain, once the first link between God and humanity was broken, all contingent links became uncoupled.

And we are broken. As Kayne West raps, "And I don't think there's nothing I can do to right my wrongs…I wanna talk to God but I'm afraid cause we ain't spoke in so long …." West's lyrics speak of the separation that sin brings to our lives. And according to the Bible, this separation is more than just lyrics in a rap song. It has deadly consequences.

**Our Sins have Separated us
from God's Love**

Our rebellion (sin) has created a wall of separation between God and us (see Isaiah 59:2). In the Scriptures, "separation" means spiritual death. And spiritual death means being completely separated from the light and life of God.

"But wait a minute," you might say. "Didn't God know all of that before He made us?

Why didn't He see that His plan was doomed for failure?" Of course, an all-knowing God would realize that we would rebel and sin. In fact, it is our failure that makes His plan so mind-blowing. This brings us to the reason that God came to Earth in human form. And even more incredible—the remarkable reason for his death.

WHAT JESUS SAID ABOUT HIMSELF

God's Perfect Solution

Author Ray Stedman writes of God's promised Messiah: "From the very beginning of the Old Testament, there is a sense of hope and expectation, like the sound of approaching footsteps: *Someone is coming!*...That hope increases throughout the prophetic record as prophet after prophet declares yet another tantalizing hint: *Someone is coming!*"[10]

The ancient prophets had foretold that a Messiah would come and be God's perfect sin offering, satisfying his justice. This perfect man would qualify to die for us. According to the New Testament authors, the only reason Jesus was qualified to die for the rest of us is because, as God, he lived a morally perfect life and wasn't subject to sin's judgment.

It's difficult to understand how Jesus' death paid for our sins. Perhaps a judicial analogy might clarify how Jesus solves the dilemma of God's perfect love and justice.

Imagine entering a courtroom, guilty of murder (you have some serious issues). As you approach the bench, you realize that

the judge is your father. Knowing that he loves you, you immediately begin to plead, "Dad, just let me go!"

To which he responds, "I love you, son, but I'm a judge. I can't simply let you go."

He is torn. Eventually he bangs the gavel down and declares you guilty. Justice cannot be compromised, at least not by a judge. But because he loves you, he steps down from the bench, takes off the robe, and offers to pay the penalty for you. And in fact, he takes your place in the electric chair.

This is the picture painted by the New Testament. God stepped down into human history, in the person of Jesus Christ, and went to the electric chair (read: cross) instead of us, for us. Jesus is not a third-party whipping boy, taking our sins, but rather he is God himself. Put more bluntly, God had two choices: to judge sin in us or to assume the punishment himself. In Christ, He chose the latter.

Although U2's Bono doesn't pretend to be a theologian, he accurately states the reason for Jesus' death:

> The point of the death of Christ is that Christ took on the sins of the world, so that what we put out did not come back to us, and that our sinful nature does not reap the obvious death. That's the point. It should keep us humbled. It's not our own good works that get us through the gates of Heaven.[11]

Jesus didn't say he was *a way* to God. He said he was *the way*, and that his death was the only solution for our sins (John 14:6).

Those who believe all religions are the same deny we have a sin problem. They refuse to take Christ's words seriously. They say God's love will accept all of us, regardless what we have done. Perhaps Hitler is deserving of judgment, they reason, but not them or others who live "decent lives". It's like saying that God grades on the curve, and everybody who gets a D- or better will get in. But this presents a dilemma.

As we have seen, sin is the absolute opposite of God's holy character. Thus we have offended the one who created us, and loved us enough to sacrifice His very Son for us. In a sense our rebellion is like spitting in His face. Neither good deeds, religion, meditation, or Karma can pay the debt our sins have incurred.

According to theologian R. C. Sproul, Jesus alone is the one who can pay that debt. He writes,

> Moses could mediate on the law; Muhammad could brandish a sword; Buddha could give personal counsel; Confucius could offer wise sayings; but none of these men was qualified to offer an atonement for the sins of the world. ... Christ alone is worthy of unlimited devotion and service.[12]

A Gift Undeserved

The biblical term to describe God's free forgiveness through Christ's sacrificial death is grace. Whereas mercy saves us from what we deserve, the grace of God gives us what we don't deserve. Let's review for a minute how Christ has done for us what we could not do for ourselves:

A NEW COSMIC CHAPTER

The new life emerging from receiving Christ and his death for sin is described as "eternal life." A forgiven and transformed life is something graspable; it is the story line of countless movies and biographies. But the idea of "eternal life" is temporally disorienting—a transformed life that goes on forever. While to think of living beyond death is both a powerful and freeing concept, it brings with it fears of the unknown.

Will we lose our identities and freedom? Will our dwelling be a cumulus cloudbank? Will we be bored?

C. S. Lewis noted that Jesus' resurrection opens a radically new chapter in the cosmic scheme of the universe.[13] Lewis also provides a helpful analogy in regard to the unknown of eternal life, stating that if a small child were told that the sexual act was the highest bodily pleasure, he would probably ask if you ate chocolate at the same time. If told no, the child would only think of sexuality in terms of negation, that it was "chocolateless." He would see sexuality as less desirable than what he knows, when in fact it is abundantly more. So, said Lewis, are our concepts of heaven and eternal life; we will see them only as negations of earth rather than what they are, abundantly more.[14]

Dr. Randy Alcorn, who has spent 25 years researching Bible passages on heaven and has taught postgraduate courses on the subject, provides an insightful account of the afterlife in his book (appropriately titled) *Heaven*.

Alcorn describes heaven as "a bright, vibrant, and physical New Earth, free from sin, suffering, and death, and brimming with Christ's presence, wondrous natural beauty, and the richness of human culture as God intended it."

Alcorn compares our experience in heaven to that of a child whose imagination is set loose. We will be "real people with real bodies enjoying close relationships with God and each other, eating, drinking, working, playing, traveling, worshiping, and discovering."[15]

Although Alcorn bases his views on several scriptures, one verse sums it up:

No eye has seen, no ear has heard,
and no mind has imagined
what God has prepared
for those who love him.
(1 Corinthians 2:9. NLT)

- *God loves us and created us for a relationship with Himself* [16]
- *We have been given the freedom to accept or reject that relationship* [17]
- *Our sin and rebellion against God and His laws have created a wall of separation between us and Him* [18]
- *Though we are deserving of eternal judgment, God has paid our debt in full by Jesus' death in our place, making eternal life with Him possible* [19]

Bono gives us his perspective on grace. "Grace defies reason and logic. Love interrupts, if you like, the consequences of your actions, which in my case is very good news indeed, because I've done a lot of stupid stuff....I'd be in big trouble if Karma was going to finally be my judge.... It doesn't excuse my mistakes, but I'm holding out for Grace. I'm holding out that Jesus took my sins onto the Cross, because I know who I am, and I hope I don't have to depend on my own religiosity."[20]

We now have the picture of God's plan of the ages coming together. But there still is one missing ingredient. According to the New Testament, each of us individually must respond to the free gift Jesus offers us. He won't force us to take it.

YOU CHOOSE THE ENDING

Author and international lecturer, Ravi Zacharias states, "Jesus' message reveals that every individual, whether Jew or Greek or Roman or from any other civilization, comes to know God not by virtue of birth, but by a conscious choice to let Him have His rule in his or her individual life."[21]

Our choices are often influenced by others. The following true story illustrates how well-intended advice can sometimes result in tragic consequences.

One man who was on the 92nd floor of the south tower of the World Trade Center had just heard a jet crashing into the north tower. Stunned by the explosion, he called the police for instructions on what to do. "We need to know if we need to get out of here, because we know there's an explosion," he said urgently on the phone.

The voice on the other end advised him not to evacuate. "I would wait 'til further notice."

"All right," the caller said. "Don't evacuate." He then hung up.

Shortly after 9:00 A.M., another jet crashed into the 80th floor of the south tower. Nearly all 600 people in the top floors of the south tower perished. The failure to evacuate the building was one of the day's great tragedies.[22]

Those 600 people perished because they relied on the wrong information, even though it was given by a person who was trying to help. The tragedy would not have occurred had the 600 victims been given the right information.

Our conscious choice about Jesus is infinitely more important than the one facing the ill-informed 9/11 victims. Eternity is at stake. We can choose one of three different responses. We can ignore him. We can reject him. Or, we can accept him.

The reason many people go through life ignoring God is that they are too busy pushing their own agenda. Chuck Colson was like that. At age 39, Colson occupied the office next to the president of the United States. He was the "tough guy" of the Nixon White House, the "hatchet man" who could make the hard decisions. Yet, in 1972, the Watergate scandal ruined his reputation and his world became unglued. Later he writes,

"I had been concerned with myself. I had done this and that, I had achieved, I had succeeded and I had given God none of the credit, never once thanking Him for any of His gifts to me. I had never thought of anything being 'immeasurably superior' to myself, or if I had in fleeting moments thought about the infinite power of God, I had not related Him to my life."[23]

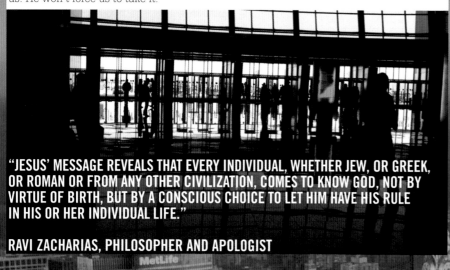

"JESUS' MESSAGE REVEALS THAT EVERY INDIVIDUAL, WHETHER JEW, OR GREEK, OR ROMAN OR FROM ANY OTHER CIVILIZATION, COMES TO KNOW GOD, NOT BY VIRTUE OF BIRTH, BUT BY A CONSCIOUS CHOICE TO LET HIM HAVE HIS RULE IN HIS OR HER INDIVIDUAL LIFE."

RAVI ZACHARIAS, PHILOSOPHER AND APOLOGIST

Many can identify with Colson. It's easy to get caught in the fast pace of life and have little or no time for God. Yet ignoring God's gracious offer of forgiveness has the same dire consequences as outright rejection. Our sin debt would still remain unpaid.

In criminal cases, few ever turn down a full pardon. In 1915, George Burdick, city editor for the *New York Tribune*, had refused to reveal sources and broken the law. President Woodrow Wilson declared a full pardon to Burdick, which he surprisingly rejected. The Supreme Court ruled that for a pardon to be valid, it must be accepted. Thus Burdick's rejection held.

Rejection of Christ's full pardon occurs for several reasons. Some use intellectual reasons, but fail to investigate the evidence. Others refuse to look beyond some hypocritical Christians they know, pointing to unloving or inconsistent behavior as an excuse. Still others reject Christ because they blame God for some sad or tragic experience they have suffered. However, Zacharias, who has lectured on hundreds of college campuses has observed a deeper reason.

"A man rejects God neither because of intellectual demands nor because of the scarcity of evidence. A man rejects God because of moral resistance that refuses to admit his need for God."[24]

C. S. Lewis recognized that his own desire for moral freedom had put him at war with God, a war he couldn't win by simply changing his behavior. Lewis compares our acceptance of Christ with that of a defeated enemy surrendering his arms:

Fallen man is not simply an imperfect creature who needs improvement: he is a rebel who must lay down his arms. Laying down your arms, surrendering, saying you are sorry, realizing that you have been on the wrong track and getting ready to start life over again….is what Christians call repentance.[25]

Repentance is a word that means a dramatic turn-around in thinking. That's what happened to Nixon's former "hatchet man". After Watergate was exposed, Colson began thinking about life differently. Sensing his own lack of purpose, he began reading Lewis's *Mere Christianity*, given to him by a friend. Trained as a lawyer, Colson took out a yellow legal pad and began writing down Lewis's arguments. Colson recalled,

I knew the time had come for me. … Was I to accept without reservations Jesus Christ as Lord of my life? It was like a gate before me. There was no way to walk around it. I would step through, or I would remain outside. A 'maybe' or 'I need more time' was kidding myself.

After an inner struggle, this former aide to the president of the United States finally realized that Jesus Christ was deserving of his full allegiance. He writes,

And so early Friday morning, while I sat alone staring at the sea I love, words I had not been certain I could understand or say fell naturally from my lips: 'Lord Jesus, I believe You. I accept You. Please come into my life. I commit it to You.'[26]

Colson discovered that his questions, "Who am I?" "Why am I here?" and "Where am I going?" are all answered in a personal relationship with Jesus Christ. The apostle Paul writes, "It is in Christ that we find out who we are and what we are living for."
(Ephesians 1:11, The Message)

When we enter into a personal relationship with Jesus Christ, he fills our inner void, gives us peace, and satisfies our desire for meaning and hope. And we no longer need to resort to temporary stimuli for our fulfillment. When He enters into us, he also satisfies our deepest longings and needs for true, lasting love and security.

And the staggering thing is that God Himself came as a man to pay our entire debt. Therefore, no longer are we under the penalty of *sin*. Paul states this clearly to the Romans when he writes,

You were his enemies, separated from him by your evil thoughts and actions, yet now he has brought you back as his friends. He has done this through his death on the cross in his own human body. As a result, he has brought you into the very presence of God, and you are holy and blameless as you stand before him without a single fault.
(Colossians 2:21b-22a NLT)

His gift of eternal life is absolutely free— and it is for the taking. The choice is yours.

End Notes

1 http://www.azlyrics.com/lyrics/ kanyewest/jesuswalks.html

2 Jack Nicholson, interviewed by Mike Sager, *Esquire*, "The Meaning of Life," (January, 2004), 70, 71.

3 *O: The Oprah Magazine*, "Oprah talks to Madonna," (January, 2004), 120.

4 Quoted in Josh McDowell, *The Resurrection Factor* (San Bernardino, CA: Here's Life Publ., 1981), 1.

5 Quoted in William R. Bright, *Jesus and the Intellectual* (San Bernardino, CA: Here's Life Publ., 1968), 33.

6 Quoted in Rick Warren, *The Purpose Driven Life* (Grand Rapids, MI: Zondervan, 2002), 17.

7 Quoted in Michka Assayas, *Bono in Conversation* (New York: Riverhead Books, 2005), 203.

8 Søren Kierkegarrd, *Philosophical Fragments*, trans. Howard V. Hong and Edna H. Hong (Princeton, NJ: Princeton University Press, 1985), 26-28.

9 C. S. Lewis, *Mere Christianity* (San Francisco: Harper, 2001), 160.

10 Ray C. Stedman, *God's Loving Word* (Grand Rapids, MI: Discovery House, 1993), 50.

11 Quoted in Assayas, 204.

12 R. C. Sproul, *Reason to Believe* (Grand Rapids, MI: Lamplighter, 1982), 44.

13 C. S. Lewis, *The Best of C. S. Lewis* (Washington, DC: Canon, 1974), 343.

14 Lewis, 357.

15 Randy Alcorn, *Heaven* (Wheaton, IL: Tyndale, 2004).

16 John 3:16; Ephesians 1:3-11

17 Genesis 3:6,7; Romans 5:12; John 3:19

18 Romans 3:23; Isaiah 59:2

19 Romans 5:15-21; Romans 6:23; Titus 3:5-7

20 Quoted in Assayas, 204.

21 Ravi Zacharias, *Jesus among Other Gods* (Nashville: Word, 2000), 158.

22 Martha T. Moore and Dennis Cauchon, "Delay Meant Death on 9/11," *USA Today*, Sept. 3, 2002, 1A.

23 Charles W. Colson, *Born Again* (Old Tappan, NJ: Chosen, 1976), 114.

24 Ravi Zacharias, *A Shattered Visage: The Real Face of Atheism* (Grand Rapids, MI: Baker, 2004), 155.

25 Lewis, Mere Christianity, 56.

26 Colson, 129.

27 Ibid., 130.

Return of the King

In J.R.R. Tolkien's, *Lord of the Rings: The Return of the King*, the mythical land of Gondor is overrun by the orcs of Mordor. Aragorn must realize his true identity and purpose as the King of Men, in order that the final battle against evil can be won.

The roots of Tolkien's plot of a returning king who destroys evil and restores peace to the world is taken from Jesus Christ's words spoken to his followers. On several occasions he had told them that he would return when the time was right. They expected it to be soon, but it has now been nearly 2,000 years since Jesus left the Earth. Jesus had a job for his followers to do before he returned.

Most Jews were bitterly disappointed by Jesus. The Messiah they wanted would conquer their enemies, and restore national prominence to Israel. The prophets had spoken of the Messiah as a coming king to rule over Israel's enemies. Five hundred years before Jesus was born the prophet Zechariah had written,

> This is what the Lord Almighty says…I am returning to Mount Zion, and I will live in Jerusalem. Then Jerusalem will be called the Faithful City; the mountain of the Lord Almighty will be called the Holy Mountain. (Zechariah 8: 2a, 3, NLT)

After Jesus' resurrection, he spent 40 days with his disciples, teaching them what they would need to know to carry on his message in a hostile world. During this time he reiterated to them that he would someday return to set up his kingdom, just as the prophets had promised. What he didn't tell them was when. Jesus did say that although no man would know the day or the hour of his return, that there would be signs when that event was drawing near. One sign would be the return of the Jews to their homeland of Israel.

As Jesus left the Earth after those 40 days, he was lifted up into the clouds. As the disciples were gazing up at what must have been an incredible sight, some angels appeared and began speaking to them. They told the disciples,

> Men of Galilee, why are you standing here staring at the sky? Jesus has been taken away from you into heaven. And someday, just as you saw him go, he will return! (Acts 1:11, NLT)

And, we are still waiting. Peter said that "in the last days" people would give up on the idea of Jesus returning. Yet, events in the world, particularly Jerusalem and the Middle East, seem to be moving towards a conclusion that only the Creator will be able to resolve. Scripture tells us that when the Jews see Jesus returning in the clouds, they will recognize their tragic mistake of rejecting him, and weep bitterly:

> They will look on me whom they have pierced and mourn for him as for an only son. They will grieve bitterly for him as for a firstborn son who has died. (Zechariah 12:10, NLT)

In Revelation, the last book of the New Testament, the apostle John summarizes the cataclysmic events that will culminate in Jesus' return. Turmoil in Jerusalem will bring the world to the brink of destruction. The world will be hopeless without God's intervention.

Those who oppose Jesus at his return will be terrified. Those who have trusted in him will be looking for him with joy and anticipation. And, prior to his return, they will be taken up to meet him in the clouds. Are we nearing the day when the return of the real King will occur?

QUESTIONS ABOUT JESUS

Q. HOW DO WE KNOW JESUS REALLY EXISTED?

A. By examining the evidence. No reputable scholar really doubts Jesus' existence. Even his enemies never attempted to dismiss him as a myth. Jesus was a real person whose life and historical impact is irrefutable. In fact, according to leading historians, no one has had a greater impact on our world than Jesus. (See article 1)

Q. COULD JESUS HAVE BEEN MERELY A GOOD MORAL TEACHER OR RELIGIOUS LEADER?

A. According to C. S. Lewis, that would be a logical impossibility. Jesus claimed equality with God. If he lied, he wouldn't have been either good or moral. If he told the truth, his claim to be God would be valid. And if he is God, Jesus couldn't have been merely a moral teacher or religious leader. (See article 2)

Q. WAS *THE DA VINCI CODE* THEORY RIGHT ABOUT JESUS' DIVINITY BEING AN "INVENTION" OF CONSTANTINE AND THE EARLY CHURCH?

A. The evidence clearly shows otherwise. His Jewish enemies had him killed because "he made himself to be God." The apostles, most of whom were eyewitnesses, regarded him as God. Even secular history acknowledges that Jesus' followers believed he was God, and openly called him "Lord" at least 200 years before Constantine. (See article 3)

Q. WERE JESUS AND MARY MAGDALENE SECRETLY MARRIED?

A. Nothing in recorded history suggests that Mary and Jesus were married or had a child. *The Da Vinci Code* points to an obscure verse in the Gnostic Gospel of Philip (written over 150 years after his death) that states Jesus kissed Mary Magdalene. This could not have been an eyewitness account. But even if was true, such expressions of friendship in first century Israel were customary. Scholars overwhelmingly dismiss a marital relationship between Jesus and Mary Magdalene as a way to sell books and increase movie box office attendance. (See article 3)

Q. HAS THE DISCOVERY OF THE GNOSTIC GOSPELS, SUCH AS THE GOSPEL OF THOMAS, PERSUADED SCHOLARS THAT THE NEW TESTAMENT ACCOUNT OF JESUS IS BAD HISTORY?

A. The New Testament presents eyewitness reports of Jesus which were readily accepted as truth by the first Christians. The Gnostic writings, on the other hand, were written 110-300 Years after Christ by unknown authors who fraudulently named them after the apostles. All the evidence supports the validity of the New Testament accounts of Jesus' life and words. (See articles 3 & 4)

Q. WHAT EVIDENCE IS THERE THAT THE NEW TESTAMENT ACCOUNT OF JESUS IS RELIABLE?

A. The New Testament is the most critically scrutinized book in history, yet its reliability has been substantiated by its early dating, number of copies, internal credibility, and extra-biblical evidence. Even if all its ancient copies were lost, virtually its entire message could still be reproduced by other letters and historical documents. (See article 4)

Q. DID JESUS FULFILL ANCIENT PROPHECIES THAT PRE-DATED HIS APPEARANCE?

A. Nearly 300 references to 61 specific prophecies from the Hebrew Old Testament were fulfilled by Jesus. These prophecies were written over 500 years before Jesus, and spell out such details as his divinity, lineage, birthplace, betrayal, crucifixion, and his mission. The odds against one person fulfilling all of these prophecies are prohibitive. (See article 5)

Q. WHAT EVIDENCE IS THERE FOR JESUS' RESURRECTION?

A. The empty tomb, the sudden rise of Christianity and the transformed behavior of Jesus' followers are unexplainable without the resurrection having been a reality. Even skeptical scholars can't explain why all of his disciples would be willing to undergo torture and martyrdom for a lie. Without the resurrection, Christianity would have been squelched by Jesus' enemies and the massive power of Rome. (See article 6)

Q. IF JESUS IS GOD, WHY DID HE SUFFER AND DIE ON THE CROSS?

A. Jesus told his followers that it is because of God's great love for us. Jesus' death was the only sacrifice acceptable to God as payment for our sins. His death paid for everyone's sins, past, present, and future. Yet this free gift must be personally received by faith, or we remain unforgiven. (See article 7)

Q. HOW DO WE KNOW JESUS CHRIST IS THE ONLY WAY TO GOD?

A. 1) Jesus said he was the only way. (See article 2)
2) His resurrection substantiates his divinity, and thus his claims. (See article 6)
3) His fulfillment of prophecy proves that he speaks for God. (See article 5)
4) The eyewitness reports bear record that his claims are true. (See article 4)
5) Jesus alone brings meaning, purpose, and hope to life. (See article 7)

QUOTES

ALBERT EINSTEIN, PHYSICIST (1879–1955)

"As a child I received instruction both in the Bible and in the Talmud. I am a Jew, but I am enthralled by the luminous figure of the Nazarene. … No one can read the Gospels without feeling the actual presence of Jesus. His personality pulsates in every word. No myth is filled with such life."

SHOLEM ASCH, JEWISH AUTHOR (1880–1957)

"Jesus Christ is to me the outstanding personality of all time, all history, both as Son of God and as Son of Man. Everything he ever said or did has value for us today and that is something you can say of no other man, dead or alive. There is no easy middle ground to stroll upon. You either accept Jesus or reject him."

PAUL, APOSTLE OF JESUS CHRIST, 62 A.D.

"Christ is the visible expression of the invisible God. He existed before creation began, for it was through Him that everything was made, whether spiritual or material, seen or unseen....Life from nothing began through Him, and life from the dead began through Him, and He is, therefore, justly called the Lord of all....It was in Him that the full nature of God chose to live...."

[Colossians 1: 15-19 J. B. Phillips]

MALCOLM MUGGERIDGE, BRITISH JOURNALIST (1903–90)

"It was while I was in the Holy Land for the purpose of making three B.B.C. television programmes on the New Testament that a...certainty seized me about Jesus' birth, ministry and Crucifixion.... there really had been a man, Jesus, who was also God."

C. S. LEWIS, OXFORD STUDENT [1898-1963] IN 1916 STATED:

"You ask me my religious views... I think, that I believe in no religion. There is absolutely no proof for any of them, and from a philosophical standpoint Christianity is not even the best. All religions, that is, all mythologies... are merely man's own invention – Christ as much as Loki."

C. S. LEWIS, OXFORD PROFESSOR IN 1952 STATED:

"If you are looking for something super-personal, something more than a person, then it is not a question of choosing between the Christian idea and other ideas. The Christian idea is the only one on the market.... Christ is the son of God."

H. G. WELLS, BRITISH AUTHOR (1866–1946)

"I am an historian, I am not a believer, but I must confess as a historian that this penniless preacher from Nazareth is irrevocably the very center of history. Jesus Christ is easily the most dominant figure in all history."

MAHATMA GANDHI, INDIAN POLITICAL LEADER (1869–1948)

"A man who was completely innocent, offered himself as a sacrifice for the good of others, including his enemies, and became the ransom of the world. It was a perfect act."

G. K. CHESTERTON, ENGLISH CRITIC AND AUTHOR (1874–1936)

"Christianity is the only religion on earth that has felt that omnipotence made God incomplete. Christianity alone has felt that God, to be wholly God, must be a rebel as well as a king."

PINCHAS LAPIDE, ORTHODOX JEWISH SCHOLAR, GERMANY (BORN 1922)

"I accept the resurrection of Easter Sunday not as an invention of the community of disciples, but as a historical event. If the resurrection of Jesus from the dead on that Easter Sunday were a public event which had been made known … not only to the 530 Jewish witnesses but to the entire population, all Jews would have become followers of Jesus."

LENNY BRUCE, AMERICAN SATIRIST (1925–1966)

"If Jesus had been killed 20 years ago, Catholic school children would be wearing little electric chairs around their necks instead of crosses."

HANS KÜNG, GERMAN THEOLOGIAN (BORN 1928)

"After the fall of so many gods in this century, this person, broken at the hands of his opponents and constantly betrayed through the ages by his adherents, is obviously still for innumerable people the most moving figure in the long history of mankind."

JOHN LENNON, BRITISH MUSICIAN [1940-1980]

"We're more popular than Jesus Christ now. I don't know which will go first; rock and roll or Christianity."

PHILIP SCHAFF, CHURCH HISTORIAN, [1819-1893]

"This Jesus of Nazareth, without money and arms, conquered more millions than Alexander, Caesar, Mohammad, and Napoleon; without science and learning, He shed more light on things human and divine than all philosophers and scholars combined...He set more pens in motion... than the whole army of great men of ancient and modern times."

AUGUSTINE OF HIPPO, CHRISTIAN THEOLOGIAN (354-430 AD)

"I have read in Plato and Cicero sayings that are very wise and very beautiful; but I never read in either of them: "Come unto me all ye that labour and are heavy laden.""

JEAN-JACQUES ROUSSEAU, PHILOSOPHER [1712-1778]

"...if the life and death of Socrates are those of a philosopher, the life and death of Jesus Christ are those of a God."

MARTIN LUTHER KING JR., AMERICAN CIVIL RIGHTS LEADER (1929–1968)

"Jesus Christ was an extremist for love, truth and goodness."

NAPOLEON BONAPARTE, FRENCH EMPEROR (1769–1821)

"Alexander, Caesar, Charlemagne, and I founded great empires. But upon what did the creation of our genius depend? Upon force. Jesus alone founded his empire upon love, and to this very day millions would die for him."

RESOURCES

JESUS UNDER FIRE:
MODERN SCHOLARSHIP
REINVENTS THE
HISTORICAL JESUS

MICHAEL F. WILKINS & J. P. MO-
RELAND, GENERAL EDITORS
ZONDERVAN, 1996,
254 PAGES

Ten highly regarded scholars address the
furor surrounding Jesus Christ, treating
such issues as his historicity and the validity of his claims, his miracles, and his resurrection. In particular, this book addresses
the skeptical claims of the Jesus Seminar,
exposing their work as an attack on the historical Jesus, rather than a search for truth.

For those who want to understand the
historical basis for Jesus in the light of scru-
tiny and skepticism, this book is essential.

JESUS AMONG OTHER
GODS: THE ABSOLUTE
CLAIMS OF THE
CHRISTIAN MESSAGE

RAVI ZACHARIAS
W PUBLISHING, 2000,
240 PAGES

The author, a Christian philosopher and
apologist, examines the difference between
Jesus and other gods and religious leaders.
Having been born in India, Zacharias is
especially well versed about the other religions laying claim to truth. His insightful
comparison of Jesus with Buddha, Muhammad, and other religious leaders establishes
the groundwork in the debate about Jesus'
uniqueness.

In the book, Zacharias exposes the futility
of Islam, Hinduism and Buddhism, when
it comes to discovering absolute truth and
meaning to life. He also highlights his own
journey from despair and meaninglessness
to the discovery that Jesus is the ultimate
source for both truth and meaning to life.

THE GOOD LIFE:
SEEKING PURPOSE, MEAN-
ING, AND TRUTH IN YOUR
LIFE

CHARLES COLSON WITH
HAROLD FICKETT
TYNDALE HOUSE, 2005,
365 PAGES

What brings happiness? Material things
such as a big house or car? Fame or suc-
cess? That's happiness! Or is it? Exploring
the ways we seek pleasure and content-
ment, Colson shares real-life stories about
people who define themselves by their
positions and possessions versus those who
discover ultimate meaning through faith in
God.

This book is written in an easy-to-read,
entertaining style, with numerous stories
and illustrations that hold reader interest.
The author writes, "This book is for seekers-
-seekers of any kind, of any or no religious
faith." The author hopes that through reading this book, seekers will find new purpose
and meaning for their lives...and according
to Colson, that is truly "the good life."